The Naked Truth About Cap d'Agde

The Naked Truth About Cap d'Agde

Making the most of a holiday
in Southern France's celebrated naked city

By Ross Velton

Scarlett, Oh!
PUBLISHING

ISBN: 0-9662683-4-2

First printing: April 2003
Book cover design: No. 9 Design, Inc., Chicago

Scarlett, Oh! Publishing
P.O. Box 6584
Villa Park, IL 60181-6584 USA
888-883-9040 (24-hour toll-free book orders; Canada and USA)
E-mail: Books@wordcrafting.com
http://www.wordcrafting.com

Scarlett, Oh! Publishing makes this book available for individual and bulk purchases. See back of book for information.

Printed in the United States of America.

Contents

Acknowledgement

To even scrape the surface of what makes Cap d'Agde tick would not have been possible without the help of the people who have made the resort what it is today. The author's greatest debt of gratitude is to Marie-Thérèse and Jean-Luc, whose lasting friendship is proof that Cap d'Agde encounters do not necessarily have to be superficial and fleeting. Their hospitality, generosity, and encouragement were appreciated enormously.

Who would have thought that on a nudist beach known for its quick love a meeting with a girl would have stirred such strong emotions? The bittersweet experience with Françoise was motivating, distracting, but never dull. Thank you for the feelings you inspired.

Thanks also to Chris for having the vision and courage to publish this book.

The following people should be acknowledged for their help, advice, and insights about why Cap d'Agde is so special for them: Gerda and Piet, Tamara and Joel, Couples Contre le Sida, Nicole and Jacky, Claudine and Jean-Paul, Annie and Eddy, Tracy and Michael, Ann and David, Renate, Isa, Fabie, Jean-René, and Kumar.

Introduction

Whether you're after sun, sea, sex, a game of pétanque, a 20-person orgy, or a ring through your penis, this guide to Cap d'Agde is for you. It will titillate the armchair traveller, educate the novice, and bring happy memories flooding back to those who have already been lucky enough to spend a week or two in—well, Paradise.

'Paradise on Earth' means different things to different people. Hedonists want perfect weather, sandy beaches, and beautiful people. Bohemians talk fancifully about a tolerant land where they can be what they want to be. Libertines dream of a place where they can boast, in all honesty, that they've had as many women or men as hot dinners. And lawyers simply want to merge, unnoticed into the crowd. The nudist resort in Cap d'Agde may not be Utopia, but for hedonists, bohemians, libertines, lawyers, and a great many others, it comes pretty close.

This book explains why Cap d'Agde has acquired mythical status for naturists, swingers, fetishists, gays, frustrated glamour queens, lonely men in raincoats, and other people from all over Europe and beyond. In the height of summer the nudist resort attracts some 60,000 people, so chances are high that you know somebody who knows somebody who's been there. And once you've heard their stories—and read this guide—there's an even better chance that you'll want to see it all for yourself.

—Ross Velton

About This Book

So much has been written about Cap d'Agde, especially in the French media, that separating fact from fiction has become difficult. Every effort has been made to give as accurate an account as possible, using information gleaned from personal experience and from people who have, in some cases, been visiting the Cap for many years. Little attempt has been made to glamorise or overexaggerate what you can expect to find and, although the opinions expressed in this book are personal, the author has made every effort to remain faithful to his guiding principle: to tell the (naked) truth.

Most of the research for this book was done during the 2002 season. The prices and other practical information were correct at the time of writing.

When the author refers to 'Cap d'Agde' or 'the Cap', unless otherwise stated, he is talking about the nudist resort (variously described in French as the 'quartier naturiste', 'village naturiste', 'camp naturiste', or 'zone naturiste') on the northeastern edge of town, and not Cap d'Agde itself—which is a large (clothed) resort town in its own right.

This book uses the metric system for measurements. Here are some of the equivalencies for American readers:

1 kilometre (2km) = 0.62 miles (2km = 1.25 miles)

1 metre (1m) = 39.37 inches (just over a yard)

1 kilogram = 2.2 pounds

1 litre = 0.9 quart (4 litres are just under a gallon)

Temperatures are provided in Celsius. To convert a Celsius temperature into Fahrenheit, multiply a Celsius temperature by 9, divide by 5, and add 32. For example, 20°C = 68°F and 25°C = 77°F.

This book uses a 24-hour clock for time, except in direct quotes. For example, 20.00 is 8 p.m.

Cap d'Agde at a Glance

The *quartier naturiste* of Cap d'Agde is one of the largest nudist resorts in the world, a popular place for naturists and sexually liberated adults alike.

Pronunciation: *Cap* (what goes on your head) + *dagged* (one syllable).

Location: The *quartier naturiste* is on the northeastern edge of the town of Cap d'Agde, which is on the Mediterranean coast of France in the *département* of Hérault in the *région* of Languedoc and Roussillon.

Size: The nudist resort is the size of a small town, bordered by a 2km-long stretch of beach.

Population: Expect a total of around 300,000 people during the entire season. In the height of summer, as many as 60,000 people visit the resort at any one time.

Infrastructure: Within the nudist resort is a beach, port, campsite, apartment complexes, hotel, shops, restaurants, bars, post office, bank, petrol station, launderettes, hairdressers, tennis courts, and other such facilities.

Climate: Expect a Mediterranean climate: mild, rainy winters and hot, dry summers.

Time: GMT + 1 hour.

Money: Euro = 100 euro cents.

Season: Mid-March to mid-October.

Chapter 1

Cap d'Agde in Context

The prospect of taking your holiday in a resort the size of a small town, where people go about their daily tasks in the nude, take their children to the beach in the afternoon, partake of a pastis and a convivial game of pétanque in the early evening, and have group sex in the clubs at night is bound to raise questions—not to mention eyebrows.

What kind of place is this? An oversized Club Med? A summer camp for seniors reliving misspent youths—and youths misspending young adulthoods? The largest den of iniquity yet known to man?

The answer has to be 'all and none of the above'. For Cap d'Agde represents different things to different people, and accurately describing what type of holiday you should expect depends on what you want to expect. Perhaps the best advice, then, for those visiting Cap d'Agde for the first time is to be ready for anything, but expect nothing.

Non-European visitors, and even those from the United Kingdom, might wonder how so much could be written about a place which, in the context of French holiday destinations, hardly trips off the tongue like Saint-Tropez, Nice, and Cannes.

Ask any half-serious German, Dutch, French, Belgian, Swiss, Italian, Danish, or Swedish naturists whether they have ever heard of Cap d'Agde, and they will probably think you are making fun of them. Ask if they have been there, and most will grin and nod. In continental Europe, this mildly ugly resort on a mildly attractive stretch of the Mediterranean coast about 50km southwest of the city of Montpellier in the French *région* of Languedoc and Roussillon is the principal meeting place for a large proportion of European nudists, swingers, and alternative lifestylers. Other large naked places are scattered throughout Europe—in Spain and Croatia, for example—but none has the mythical reputation enjoyed (or endured) by Cap d'Agde.

Whether the Cap is still the largest nudist community in Europe is debatable. Even so, it receives around 300,000 visitors annually, and its 120 or so businesses drive an economy worth at least 10 million euro a season.

More has been written about Cap d'Agde than any other nudist resort in the world, although unfortunately much of the press is over-sensationalised—if not plain rubbish. To explain the Cap d'Agde phenomenon to the general public, the type of journalist who probably thinks twice before taking a shower in the nude has sensationalised the place to such an extent that separating fact from fiction, myth from reality, is difficult. This fiction, of course, has done no harm to the Cap's visitor stats.

From small acorns, great sycamores grow

Visit Cap d'Agde today, and the German presence quickly becomes apparent. Whether they are dancing on the tables at the Melrose or pinching the best spots on the beach, these keen naturists have found a natural home in Cap d'Agde.

And so it was in the beginning. Around 1958, a caravanload of lost Germans arrived at a deserted stretch of beach in the south of France. (Strictly speaking, the first German arrivals were the soldiers who came to mine these parts during World War II, although presumably the nudist potential of the area was not fully appreciated at that time).

In the early 1960s, however, the nudist potential was recognised. The owners of the land upon which the Germans had stumbled were two brothers, René and Paul Oltra, winegrowers who had purchased the unpromising vineyards for the princely sum of 'one franc six sous'.

At that time, the only other nudist community in France was on the Atlantic coast at Montalivet. When the Germans returned the following year with five other vehicles, René Oltra had the idea of opening a naturist campsite on his land.

The local authorities granted the required permission, and by the end of the 1960s some bungalows and a small office at the entrance had been added to the several tents and caravans. The first brick construction began in 1971 at Port Ambonne, to be followed by Port Nature, Héliopolis, and plenty of other aesthetically dubious but functional buildings.

Jekell and Hyde: Who comes to Cap d'Agde?

No one can give a precise date when the first shaved pussy or pierced clitoris arrived in Cap d'Agde, although the clientele began to change in the early 1990s. Before then, the nudist resort was essentially just that: a place where people came to be naked, and nothing more. A fair amount of sex was always going on at the campsite, but this sex was of the husband-cheating-on-wife and wife-cheating-on-husband variety rather than swinging.

This new breed of visitor, the swingers, described in French as 'à poilistes', differed from the pure naturists in that they saw no reason to separate naturism and sex. Indeed they actively encouraged complete sexual liberty and expression, shocking the status quo but gaining grudging acceptance due to the revenue they generated.

Today some argue that the people who visit Cap d'Agde primarily for sex, in whatever form, *are* the status quo. If the Cap receives some 300,000 visitors a year, about 100,000 of these are libertines, and they account for roughly 80% of the resort's economic turnover.

First-time visitors might not notice that the Cap has an identity crisis at the moment. Is it a nudist colony? Is it a swingers resort? Can it be both? Do children have a place? Without over-analysing these philosophical questions, be aware of the Cap's split personality. But the place is large enough to enjoy your own style of holiday without too much interference from the not-so-like-minded. Just keep an open mind and be tolerant.

One of the great things about naturism is its wide-ranging appeal—its ability to attract all types from all walks of life. The Cap d'Agde nudist resort is no different. You are as likely to meet a judge as a janitor, a doctor as a doorman, a policeman as a plumber on the beach and around the resort.

'The scariest thing I ever saw at Cap d'Adge was a gardener, wearing only a short shirt, who was enthusiastically pruning the shrubbery with a power pruner. Every time he made a wide swinging sweep at the bushes I cringed,' said a man from Canada on his first trip to the Cap.

Although making a broad distinction between the naturist and the libertine clientele is possible, there are few other generalisations when describing who visits Cap d'Agde. Take the long-time resident at the campsite, for example, who used to spend hours in the showers opposite his site, looking at dirty magazines and playing with himself. One day this grey old man simply keeled over and died right there in the showers, and although many had either seen him or heard of him before, no one actually knew who he was. Turns out he was an important clergyman at the Vatican.

The brains of the famously cerebral French are, after all, in their underpants

The way in which the Cap's clientele has changed over the past 10 years has had a lot to do with what has been happening in France since the late 1960s. Always a country with a strong sexual identity, a new wind of sexual freedom swept over France in the late 1960s after student demonstrations and the fall of Charles de Gaulle. Since then, the number of establishments based in some way on sex and catering to the type of people who party in Cap d'Agde has been growing steadily, particularly in Paris. (To experience the delights of the French capital before going to the Cap, see *Warming Up in Paris* on page 40.)

Today, even the smallest French town has at least one disco, sauna, or restaurant for swingers. A cursory search of the French-speaking Web unearths hundreds of contact sites for like-minded adults.

Naturism, too, has a fine tradition in France. The Fédération Française de Naturisme (French Naturist Federation) lists some 85 nudist centres in the country, and swingers magazines cite as many non-textile beaches where exhibitionism, voyeurism, and the like are practised.

Wherever you go in France these days, you'll find something naughty to do. Perhaps France was always like this; but don't think for a moment that it has the European monopoly on sexual recreation (Germany, Belgium, and the Netherlands also are hot). But somewhere as unconventional and immoral as Cap d'Agde is appropriate in the land of sloppy tongue kisses, Brigitte Bardot's pouting lips, and the Marquis de Sade's whips.

Be a fine weather naturist

The naturist season at Cap d'Agde runs from the middle of March to the middle of October. This period is when the campsite is open for business; and several die-hard nudists invariably wait at the front gate on the morning of the Ides of March to be let in.

The weather at this time of year—as well as towards the end of the season—is not always ideal for sauntering around in the buff. Unlike the Caribbean, for example, Mediterranean France has a climate marked distinctly by the four seasons. Although late spring, summer, and early autumn are hot and sunny, the winter months are decidedly fresh by comparison, and only suitable for the type of masochist who turns out on December 31 for the annual *dernier bain naturiste de l'année* (last naked swim of the year). For the 2001 event, the air temperature was 6°C and the sea was a testicle-shrivelling 8°C.

Although Cap d'Agde is renown for its many days of sunshine, rain does happen. At least your clothes won't get wet.

Nothing stops from you renting an apartment or hotel room at the Cap in January, but hardly anything will be open and you will likely be alone in an empty playground. Good, perhaps, for writing a book about your experiences the previous summer, free from temptation and other carnal distractions, but not so good if you want to see the real Cap d'Agde.

Even at the beginning and end of the season many of the resort's businesses (restaurants, shops, bars, clubs) are closed. These closures might not bother you if you intend to be self-sufficient at the campsite and don't care too much about the Cap's frisky nightlife.

To be more or less sure that most of the resort's facilities will be open during your visit, plan your stay for some time between May and the middle of September.

On average, the Cap enjoys 267 sunny days a year. Of these, 193 occur between March and October. Note also that the wind, which locals call the Mistral (although strictly speaking the Mistral is on the eastern Mediterranean coast of France), is often quite strong and consistent. The wind can literally blow non-stop for three days. Good for flying kites, but not sunbathing on a beach with little shelter. Average maximum temperatures are as follows:

January:	19°C	July:	29°C
February:	19°C	August:	26°C
March:	21°C	September:	24°C
April:	23°C	October:	20°C
May:	24°C	November:	18°C
June:	26°C	December:	18°C

Choosing the best time for your trip

The weather is not the only factor that should influence when you choose to visit Cap d'Agde. Largely due to the police presence on the beach and the generally heightened security during the high season (see *Les Gendarmes du Cap* on page 67), the atmosphere and sexual vibe of the resort is different in June, for example, than it is in August.

Before the police arrive on July 1 and as soon as they leave some time in early September, the swingers beach is a hotbed of exhibitionist couples and voyeuristic single men (see *It's a Beach, Jim, but Not as We Know It* on page 80). The clientele at these times is usually dedicated and motivated in practising the sexual openness for which the Cap has gained a reputation. It is made up of a high proportion of German and Dutch swingers. The average age also tends to be slightly higher (40s and 50s) than it is during the high season (more 20s and 30s).

During the unpoliced periods, the European school holidays have either yet to start or have finished, which means fewer families are visiting—and therefore fewer children are around to be protected from spontaneous displays of public sex. The last two weeks in June (when the weather is usually as good as it is in July and August) is an excellent time to visit the Cap if you enjoy a sexually charged atmosphere and techniques of seduction not necessarily restricted to languorous eye contact and the incessant pluming of silicon feathers. At this time of the year, people like to touch and to be touched.

The first two weeks in September also used to be a good time for sex on the beach, but the lingering presence of the police has spoilt the fun in the past couple of years. '[In 2002] the police left on September 15. Everyone had been waiting patiently for their departure. It had been planned for September 8, but they stayed one week more. As soon as they left it was crazy,' says Arnaud from Paris (France).

The police presence on the swingers beach during high season has put a stop to all but the most innocent of physical contact. Combine this benign behaviour with the huge influx of holidaying families, and one part of the beach is much like any other at this time of year.

Gays continue to congregate on the northeastern edge of the nudist beach, and a high concentration of swingers can still be found near the Restaurant Buvette de Marseillan. But during high season these areas are meeting places rather than outdoor porn theatres.

The clientele also is slightly different in July and August. The hard-core, middle-aged German swingers and flocks of masturbating single men are less evident, usurped by a generally younger, Latin crowd. From July 15 to August 15 (the busiest time of the year), the Cap is full of French and especially Italian couples who like to strut their stuff. Although this time is ideal for meeting the beautiful people, don't automatically assume that they are there to play. Window-shopping is rife during high season and, although you will be spoilt for choice, the chances of intimacy with a couple in August are not necessarily higher than in June.

At the risk of generalising even further about the subtle changes in atmosphere during the course of a season in Cap d'Agde, here is a brief aid to choosing the best time for your trip:

Visit the Cap in May, June, or late September if:

- You don't like crowds—unless there's something naughty going on at the beach.
- You like to have sex on the beach.

- You like to watch other people have sex on the beach.
- You are not fussy about the appearance and age of the people who you are either having sex with or watching having sex.
- You are willing to sacrifice a day or two of good weather for more sexual freedom.
- You will not be shocked if a short, hairy man with a Jack Nicholson-style grin lays his yellow-stained beach towel a mere three steps from where you are rubbing suntan lotion on your partner's back and starts playing with himself in the hope that your innocent massage might lead to something more juicy.
- You will not be upset if, when you have finished applying the lotion, you discover that the man has relieved himself all over the his-and-hers John Grisham novels that you and your partner were planning to use to shield your eyes from other men of his ilk.

Visit the Cap in July and August (especially July 15 to August 15) and early September if:

- You like naked crowds.
- You have reserved your accommodation well in advance.
- You are planning a family holiday that involves children.
- You are offended by displays of public sex.
- You like to be surrounded by beautiful people, thereby optimising your chances of finding the rare couple that both you *and* your partner genuinely fancy.
- You will not be frustrated if you find that many of these beautiful people will never let you—or anyone else for that matter—get close enough to sniff their expensive perfumes, let alone stroke them.

How much does it all cost?

'[The Cap] is an expensive way to buy freedom, but it's acceptable,' say Yvon and Max from Amsterdam (Holland). This description could either mean that the price is worth paying for the freedom or, although on the expensive side,

Cap d'Agde is not exorbitant. In many ways, both are true.

You will pay more in Cap d'Agde than at many other French resort towns, and sometimes the quality of the goods and services does not justify the price. On the other hand, these costs could be seen as a necessary evil for having the opportunity to spend your holiday in such a unique place.

Besides paying living and travelling costs, you will have to eat, drink, and be merry. A meal in a restaurant costs from around 15 euro to as much as 50 or 60 euro if you opt for one of the smarter places and include wine. Drinks in the bars typically start at around 3 euro, and admission to the swingers clubs will set you back about 30 euro (for a couple).

Then add the purchases of lingerie and various leather items in the boutiques, a massage or facial at a beauty salon, drinks and ice creams or pastries on the beach, a day or two at the swimming pool, and perhaps even an excursion outside the resort, and costs mount quickly. General, everyday purchases such as groceries, toiletries, magazines, and the like are only a little more expensive than normal.

And, as Chris from Chicago (USA) can testify, some of the basic necessities can be picked up at bargain prices: 'US$1.75 for champagne? That's right! Pol Remy *demi-sec* is the cheapest sparkling wine around—and it's tasty. You can find it on the bottom shelf of some wine shops in the naturist section and occasionally the Hyper U in town [Agde] carries it. Five of us killed 57 bottles in one week because it was cheaper than anything else to drink.'

You could easily burn up 100 euro a day in the nudist resort (not including accommodation costs) if you eat out and party every night. Self-catering will save some money, as will devising your own entertainment at home.

In April 2003, the euro was worth the following amounts against other major currencies:

1 euro = 1.08 U.S. dollars

1 euro = 1,57 Canadian dollars

1 euro = 0,68 British pound

1 euro = 1,78 Australian dollars

1 euro = 1,96 New Zealand dollars

Travelling as a single

Unlike many swingers resorts—and even naturist centres with no sexual connotations attached—single men are as welcome as couples and single women in Cap d'Agde. Loners can rent an apartment, stay at the campsite, use the beach, and enjoy many, though admittedly not all, of the resort's facilities.

But what you derive from your Cap d'Agde experience depends on the people you meet and, if applicable, the person or people with whom you choose to go on holiday with. Since the former is often so dependent on the latter, the decision whether to go alone, with a partner, or in a group is crucial.

The decision regarding travel companions can only be made once you have decided why you are going to Cap d'Agde in the first place. If simply for the naturism, then going alone or with someone will have little bearing on where you can go and what you can do in the resort. Remember that, despite the complex identity it now possesses, Cap d'Agde was originally intended for naked holidaymakers, and this ethos still ultimately prevails today (at least in the tourist brochures).

You may choose to go with a partner, a friend, or in a group to save on the costs of accommodation, which is normally rented per apartment rather than per person (see *Even Naturists Need a Roof Over Their Heads* on page 48), or if you dread the thought of spending a week or two in your own company.

Other issues raise their ugly heads if your primary motive for going to the Cap is to get laid. In this case, the arguments for male visitors being joined by female companions are persuasive. First off, entry to almost all the swingers clubs—where most of the sex these days takes place—is reserved for couples and single ladies. The way you are treated

You have to go to considerable lengths to stand out in Cap d'Agde. Two naked women caressing each other in a phone box would cause heart attacks anywhere else; here, they raise no more than an eyebrow and provoke a smutty grin.

by fellow visitors also differs radically depending on whether you are alone or with a woman. Lone men are routinely treated with suspicion and, on bad days, utter contempt by couples.

Men who can show their other half, however, invariably receive a warmer welcome, even if encounters don't progress sexually. Single men considering bringing a women with them to Cap d'Agde should avoid using a female friend as a passport to enable them to enjoy activities, such as private parties and access to swingers clubs, which would be off-limits if they were alone. Spending a holiday with someone who does not want to dance to your sexual tune will probably damage the friendship.

All the above does not apply to single women. They are welcomed with open arms almost everywhere since they are so relatively thin on the ground. Sexually confident women who know what they want, and who know how to say no to people not offering what they want, will have the time of their lives in Cap d'Agde.

If, on the other hand, you are liable to be upset or intimidated by the newfound popularity of your hitherto unnoticed body, you might opt for safety in numbers or a male companion to shield you from unwanted attention (if women are sometimes used as passports, why can't men be used as insect repellent?).

Cap d'Agde regulars often arrive in groups formed over the course of past visits, once again saving on accommodation costs and guaranteeing a good ambiance even if the offering of new flesh is lame. These groups are easy to identify on the beach; becoming part of the circle will, as always, be easier for couples and single women than for single men.

Making contacts on the Web

If you have decided you would prefer to visit the Cap with someone other than Auntie Matilda, but you don't have anyone particular in mind, or you fancy the idea of arranging to meet someone when you arrive in the resort, the Web is, in principle at least, an excellent way to go about finding like-minded friends. Savvy surfers know, however, that Internet contact sites and chat rooms, especially if they have anything remotely to do with sex, can be an enormous waste of time and energy.

Single men are in for a particularly soul-destroying time. You see a profile that piques your interest, write a lengthy introductory e-mail describing your many fine qualities, attach the sexiest photo you can find, and send it all with high hopes to lolita69@sucker.com. The reply, if you ever receive one, will likely be to invite you to look at her latest XXX pictures—for a small fee, of course.

The other scenario is that you start chatting to someone who, although pleasant and open-minded, looks like the back end of a bus. Single women, on the other hand, will be inundated with replies if they advertise their desire to go on holiday to a nudist resort with a single guy. The trick here is to sort the genuine candidates from the many randy sods who don't intend to accompany you any further than the local discotheque, let alone to a far-off land where the people bathe in garlic before lunging for your crotch. To round off this pessimism, while plenty of genuine couples are looking to meet other couples on the Web, finding four people who fancy one other enough to go on holiday together is quite another story.

The Internet is most useful to let people who share the same interests as yourself know you will be in Cap d'Agde between such and such a date. Consider posting a message, preferably with a photograph that shows your face, on a contact site frequented by potential Cap d'Agde visitors. Then let interested parties contact you. If you have set your mind on scouring the Internet to find a travel companion before leaving home, keep your expectations low. Start chatting with people informally, developing a certain trust and friendship, before bringing up naturism, Cap d'Agde, and your desire to watch your, as yet virtual, friend have sex with 20 men as you jerk off. Such subjects need to be raised discreetly.

Finally, a chance to travel light?

Having selected your travel dates to coincide nicely with the warmest and sunniest weather, you might be duped into thinking that, since you will be visiting a nudist resort, almost no luggage is required. Wrong! Even if you are coming to the Cap with no other agenda than simply stripping down and being naked for 24 hours a day, you should bear one or two things in mind before leaving home with only your toothbrush.

Although Mediterranean summers are generally superb, they are not tropical and the weather can change quite abruptly. On the occasional bad day when temperatures drop to around 20°C and the wind (which is often strong) picks up, you will be grateful for a sweater, a pair of trousers, some proper shoes, and perhaps even a light coat. These items of clothing are even more relevant in the evenings, especially if you are camping.

Indeed, campers will need to bring with them the assorted paraphernalia that this activity entails. Visitors from European countries often choose to drive their RVs and caravans to Cap d'Agde, which creates less incentive for travelling light.

North American and other overseas visitors intent on camping, though, must carry their gear on their own backs. A tent, a ground mat, and a sleeping bag are probably minimum requirements if you merely want protection from the elements and a few hours of sleep a night; a more luxurious *chez-vous* involves bringing often heavy and bulky items such as gas cookers, inflatable mattresses (essential if you plan to bring people back to play under the *belle étoile*), lights, chairs, and a table. Note that the baggage allowance on most airlines is around 20 kilograms.

One frustrating aspect of renting an apartment in Cap d'Agde is that, in most cases, you must provide your own cleaning products and other such items (cooking utensils, towels, and sheets are provided). Once again, motorised visitors will be able to bring these sundries with them without much trouble; those arriving on foot will either have to make space for them in baggage, buy them when they arrive, or forget them altogether (see *Even Naturists Need a Roof Over Their Heads* on page 48).

Apart from warm, sensible clothing, other choices threaten to make that light bag cumbersomely heavy. The bane of the female suitcase is footwear. If each sexy outfit must be accompanied by a different pair of shoes of hardly Cinderella proportions (if recent trends are anything to go by) then beware. Add a pair of thigh-length PVC boots to the collection, and you will soon be dangerously close to your baggage allowance limit. To economise on the amount of foot-wear you pack, choose outfits that go with almost anything— a somewhat hollow statement, perhaps, if you are coming to the Cap precisely because you want to show off the clothes you dare not wear on Main Street, Prudesville, USA.

Sex toys, particularly, though not exclusively, for the la-dies, are other baggage bloaters. But for many women these items are as essential as a ticket and passport.

The shops in the nudist resort stock most items you would logically pack for a naturist beach holiday (suntan lotion, lip balm, shaving foam, cock rings, and the like). One or two items, however, are more tricky to find in the resort itself and are probably worth bringing with you if you don't want to waste time looking for them in the town of Cap d'Agde or, more likely, Agde itself. These items include:

- Special medication, creams, lotions, sprays—the nudist resort has only one pharmacy, so if your desired product isn't there, you must look for it in town.
- Contact lenses—although you might find cleaning fluid at the pharmacy, there is no optician where you can buy replacement lenses.
- English books and magazines—although the *tabacs* (newsagents) in the resort stock a small selection of En-glish-language newspapers and magazines (*International Herald Tribune, Time, Cosmopolitan*, and other such

mainstream titles), the vast majority of the reading matter available is in French.

- Female condoms—if you prefer this method of contraception, bring your own supply.

Note, too, that the smoking of dope and taking of other mind-altering substrances, while by no means unhead of, is not commonplace in the nudist resort. If drugs are your thing, you will have to make enquiries as to where you can get your hands on such goodies; do not expect unsolicited offers of drugs.

Veuillez-vous coucher avec moi ce soir?

Many an English speaker has left the Cap ruing the number of missed opportunities of making friends due to the ultimately insurmountable language barrier, and swearing that when they return the next year they will have an arsenal of sexy French phrases along the same lines as the famous *veuillez-vous coucher avec moi ce soir*—but hopefully a little more ingenious. Indeed, although English is your best bet if you want to communicate with the Germans, Dutch, and Scandinavians, the French, and often the Swiss, Belgians, and Italians, will prefer, if not require, you to speak or at least understand some French.

And swingers should remember that the words and phrases they have learned in order to seduce could also be used to spice up the sexual encounter itself. (Note, however, that talking dirty in French without having first mastered the pronunciation is liable to cause cries of laughter rather than ecstasy.)

A basic knowledge of French—this time the schoolboy variety—also is extremely useful out-and-about in the nudist resort, given the generally low level of English spoken in the shops, bars, and restaurants. The French shopkeepers typically respect an honest attempt at starting any conversation with French. If they know English, they'll usually switch to it when they realise from your accent, bad grammar, and limited vocabulary that you are not a native speaker. (See the appendix on page 175 for the basic standards of French and helpful naughty French phrases.)

Don't get too worried about the language barrier, though. As Chris from Chicago (USA) explains, linguistic ignorance can be bliss. 'I won't be starting up friendships or relationships with people if they don't speak English because my French is so basic. I feel as though they [the people] are a lovely backdrop to my vacation that I can watch and listen to without being directly involved with.'

FAQs

Is nudity compulsory?

Around town as many people are wearing clothes as are not, although on the beach almost everyone is naked. Indeed you will raise eyebrows if you choose to wear a swimming costume on the beach, if not protests from fellow sunbathers that you should be in the nude. Women wearing something down below are assumed to be having their period, but this textile allowance is about the only exception.

The Fédération Française de Naturisme-affiliated campsite also officially requires nudism on its premises, although this rule is loosely enforced. The great thing about Cap d'Agde is that it lacks the naturist militancy found at many other resorts, which should suit first-timers and part-time nudists.

Is everyone naked everywhere and at all times?

On the beach almost everyone is naked; nudity also is prevalent at the campsite. This *déshabillement* is not the case in the other parts of the resort—the shops, restaurants, and other businesses—where people often opt to wear at least a wrap or a swimming costume—although you have the right to be naked at any time anywhere within the confines of the resort. In the evenings, almost everyone is wearing clothes, even if sometimes the outfits are so skimpy or revealing that they hardly merit being described as such.

What should I wear?

One of the great things about Cap d'Agde is that you can wear what you want when you want. The only place where a dress code is imposed is in the swingers clubs: men should avoid wearing shorts—unless they are of the tight-fitting and provocative variety—and women in trousers are sometimes refused entry, if not to the club itself, then to the playrooms within.

Are the people on the beach all top models?

Not at all. Although certain months (August, for example) tend to attract a younger and arguably a more attractive crowd, the overwhelming majority of people who visit Cap d'Agde are imperfect creatures—in other words, normal. Cellulite, stretch marks, wrinkles, sagging breasts, and pot-bellies are nothing to be ashamed of here, where finding safety in numbers is easy. You *will* see beautiful people on the beach—they are just outnumbered by average folks.

Can we bring our children?

No one will stop you from bringing your children to Cap d'Agde. One of the reasons the police are on the beach during high season is to protect the children—who are present in great numbers during these months—from impromptu peep shows. Parents should note, however, that despite whatever the brochures might say, the Cap is a bad imitation of a family-oriented nudist resort. Activities for children extend to the beach and pool, but most of them seem to be tacked onto the money-spinning adult entertainment package.

Is this resort town a place for the disabled?

In a placed renowned for its acceptance of all comers, handicapped people should not be deterred from visiting Cap d'Agde on the basis that they will be judged. Indeed, the disabled are well represented on the beach and around town at night. They will not attract undue attention. Wheelchair users, however, will find the resort woefully lacking in making life easier. This poor access reflects the situation in the rest of France and will be most noticeable for North Americans accustomed to relatively good wheelchair access at home.

Is the naturist quarter safe?

Judging by the number of police and private security

companies patrolling the *quartier naturiste* these days, you can be forgiven for thinking that you have just arrived in the world's first naked ghetto. Although thefts (particularly on the beach), aggressive behaviour, the occasional fistfight, and other such disturbances do occur, the heightened security is really to clean up the Cap's permissive reputation. You should feel physically safe walking around the nudist resort by day or by night. Just don't wander too far from your beach bag to avoid theft.

Is it expensive?

Compared with other places along the Mediterranean coast of France such as Saint-Tropez and Cannes, Cap d'Agde is not all that expensive. Even so, prices are inflated for the tourists, and those expecting great value for their money will be disappointed. France's conversion to the euro in January 2002 has also made items more expensive. When converting prices from francs to euros businesses tended to round up the figures, sometimes by as much as 30%.

Who comes to Cap d'Agde?

When Cap d'Agde began, it was a naturist centre like all the others: perhaps not the most family-oriented place in France, but nevertheless a resort attracting huge numbers of naturists from all over Europe. Then around the early 1990s the swingers and alternative lifestylers began to arrive in force, changing the Cap's reputation forever.

Nowadays, if you believe all that is written in the press, you would think that the only people who come to Cap d'Agde are those looking for sex. Although the lifestylers are abundant and easily recognisable around town, about two-thirds of the people who visit the Cap are still only interested in the naturist side of things. Couples and single men are in the majority, with families and finally single women constituting the remainder of the clientele. This mix makes for an interesting, if not always a harmonious, group of people.

Are single men welcome?

Well-behaved, respectful, and discreet single guys are

not unwelcome. Add to this personality a good sense of humour, a decent appearance, a smattering of French, and something interesting to say, and you will quickly find your place. No one wants a rude, obnoxious man who thinks he has a God-given right to ogle, fondle, and penetrate anything that moves. The same goes for rude, obnoxious men with big dicks.

Is this a place for single women?

The answer to this question depends on the type of woman you consider yourself to be. Nymphomaniacs will love the Cap. Girls in a rut back home who want to get laid will find the place therapeutic. Open-minded, curious women who enjoy naturism and are possibly open to more if the chemistry is there—and this type is the vast majority—will enjoy much of what the Cap has to offer, even though they will occasionally have to make allowances for the perversities of human nature. Nothing dangerous here—just slightly shocking at times. On the other hand, Cap d'Agde is not for girls as pure as the driven snow, for whom making love with the lights on is a subject for the confessional and one-night stands a deadly sin.

Whatever type of person you may be, however, you will always be in great demand, not only by single men, but also couples and other bisexual women. Using this selling power to your advantage is the trick to having an unforgettable holiday in Cap d'Agde. But if you just want to read your book on the beach, you will be happy, too.

Is there a lot of prostitution?

Somewhat surprisingly, no. Even with too many horny single men to go around, professional ladies aren't on hand to deal with the overflow. Prostitution is strictly forbidden in the swingers clubs, and rarely will you see evidence of it elsewhere in the resort.

Is it gay-friendly?

Yes and no. On the one hand, a section of the beach is unofficially reserved for homosexuals, be they male or female.

Gay singles and couples inhabit many of the resort's apartments and have a significant presence at the campsite.

On the other hand, the number of facilities specifically oriented to the gay market is dwindling year on year. Apart from a bar, a club, and a couple of restaurants, few places exist where gays can go to meet like-minded people. The pickings are particularly thin for lesbians. Having said this, the Cap is an amazingly tolerant place, and people rarely feel uncomfortable on account of their sexual preferences—unless those desires are illegal.

Is sex compulsory?

Little is compulsory in Cap d'Agde. If you choose to spend your days sunbathing on the swingers beach, expect absolutely no obligation to participate in the sexual activity taking place at any given moment. Likewise, you are perfectly entitled to visit a swingers club without doing anything sexual. The chances are that you will have been invited to a private party because you have expressed an interest in playing, but even here there is no obligation. Make clear from the outset that you only want to go so far so no confusion exists.

This communication is no different from conventional dating. And though the French style of seduction can often seem quite pushy, a polite but firm 'no' or the removal of a hand from a thigh is invariably respected.

Chapter 2

Bare Essentials

As wild and unconventional as Cap d'Agde has thus far been made to seem, some routine, mundane practicalities must be addressed before you can strip off and hit the beach with a clear conscience. First you have to get there. Then you'll need to find a place to stay and learn how to keep body and soul together for the duration of your trip. And knowing some etiquette tips before your debut helps too. Then, just maybe, you'll be ready for the sometimes unreal reality of Cap d'Agde.

Getting there

Nothing is complicated about finding your way to Cap d'Agde, even if you are coming from far-off shores—except, of course, if you forget your travel documents. All overseas and non-European Union citizens require a **passport** with or without a tourist visa for France depending on your nationality. European Union citizens must have some acceptable form of photo ID (a passport or identity card is best). Citizens of the United States, Canada, Australia, and New Zealand, among other countries, do not require a visa to enter France, and they can normally stay up to 90 days.

Going with a tour operator

Visiting Cap d'Agde as part of an organised tour has advantages. You can forget about booking the flight, the transfers, the accommodation, and focus instead on making the most of your actual stay. The better tour operators will have experienced staff who know a fair amount about the place. Organised tours are also a great opportunity to meet fellow travellers with whom you will no doubt have things in common—not the least the language.

Expect to pay a pretty penny for your Cap d'Agde holiday if you are coming from North America. Tour operators in these parts specialise in Caribbean resorts, where most of the North American naturist and alternative lifestyle market are in the habit of going, and Cap d'Agde will be a bit off-the-beaten-track for most. Expect to pay around US$2,500 for a trip, which includes flights, transfers, taxes, entrance fees, and seven nights in the Cap, with a couple more nights in somewhere like Paris or Nice also part of the deal.

Better prices can be found in Europe, where Cap d'Agde is the destination of choice for thousands of nudists. Typical packages in the high season (August) with U.K.-based Peng Travel, for example, go for around US$800, which again includes flights (London–Montpellier), transfers, all taxes and entrance fees, and seven night's accommodation—but not the stopover in Paris or Nice. Note that prices drop by more than 40% in May. Tour operators with trips to Cap d'Agde are listed in *Quick Reference* on page 183.

The independent traveller

Most people visiting Cap d'Agde from European countries do not go with a tour operator. They travel down independently, normally in cars. They book their accommodation through one of the resort's rental agencies or make reservations at the campsite or hotel. Nothing stops overseas visitors from going this route as well. And although planning will take a bit more than simply booking a package with a tour operator, the effort will likely save you money and give you more flexibility. You can travel to Cap d'Agde by air or by land. (The final leg will be by car, taxi, or bus.)

Flying in

Arrivals from North America first need to buy a transatlantic flight, with Paris being the cheapest destination in France to fly to. Most major North American and European airlines have flights to Paris from various points in North America, though sometimes they require a connection in another North American or European city. Your transatlantic flight may include an onward flight to an airport closer to Cap d'Agde; enquire when making your booking to ensure the best pricing.

Transatlantic flights on scheduled airlines during high season (roughly early June to late August—which inconveniently coincides with the Cap d'Agde season) typically cost more than US$1,000. Flying during midweek and at unsociable hours could save a bit of money, as will shopping around (both at established travel agents and on the Internet) for the best deals.

Several airports are within reasonable travelling distance of Cap d'Agde. The closest is Béziers-Agde-Vias Airport, a mere 15km from the Cap and served by direct flights from Paris on **Air Littoral** (www.air-littoral.fr). A greater range of airlines fly to other nearby airports such as those at Montpellier (60km), Nîmes (110km), Carcassonne (120km), and Toulouse (215km). A return (round-trip) flight from Paris to Montpellier should not cost more than 100 euro. Every Wednesday, **Air France** (www.airfrance.fr) runs a promotion called 'Coup de Coeur', where unbooked seats on domestic flights are sold at greatly reduced prices—worth checking out if the timing is right.

The situation for those visitors arriving by air from other countries in Europe has been given a welcome boost in recent years by the emergence of the so-called low-cost or no-frills airlines. These companies offer flights at sometimes ridiculously low prices to most of the airports in southern France with quick and easy access to Cap d'Agde. For example, **Ryan Air** (www.ryanair.com) flies direct from Brussels to Carcassonne, Frankfurt to Montpellier, and London to Carcassonne, Montpellier, and Nîmes; and **Buzz** (www.buzzaway.com) serves the London–Toulouse route.

Provided that you book in advance and avoid weekend travel, one-way fares can be as low as 15 euro, with no major catches other than a slightly lower baggage allowance limit, strictly enforced check-in times, and no free in-flight food or drink. These airlines do not issue tickets; you make and pay for your reservation online or by telephone, and then turn up at the airport at the appointed time with your passport. In addition to the low-cost airlines, the vast European flight network means that you can travel to Cap d'Agde by air from nearly anywhere on the continent, although, as with the transatlantic flights, the route might not be direct.

The car versus the train

Judging by the vehicles with foreign license plates that fill the resort's car parks and campsite, **driving** is the most popular way of travelling to Cap d'Agde. Most French visitors drive to the Cap, as do those intending to camp. The advantages of having your own transport are increased flexibility, not having to worry about travelling light, and easy access to points of interest beyond the resort. Drivers should note that French roads are particularly congested during school holidays; expect longer journey times from July 15 to August 15.

The town of Agde, which is about 6.5km from Cap d'Agde, lies on the main highway or *autoroute* A9, which comes from Montpellier (and all points north) and runs parallel to the Mediterranean coast before veering south towards Perpignan and the Spanish border. Exit the highway at Agde, take *route nationale* N312 then N112 to Cap d'Agde, and follow the signs marked 'Naturisme' to the nudist resort.

You have to pay to use the *autoroutes* of France; the *route nationales*, however, are free. For example, the 1,100km-trip from the Channel port of Calais to Montpellier costs around 60 euro, and the 240km journey from Toulouse to Montpellier sets you back about 15 euro. Add to these tolls the relatively high cost of fuel in France (certainly when compared with prices in the United States), and driving to Cap d'Agde will probably not work out as the cheapest option—unless you are travelling with a full car and splitting the costs. Budget on spending not much less than 300 euro a week on **car rental.**

Apartment rentals normally include a private **parking** spot (you pay extra for a garage). If you can find a spot, you can park for free virtually anywhere in the resort. A car park is also opposite of the Welcome office (no charge), but you would then have to enter the resort on foot.

France has one of the most extensive, reliable, and comfortable **train** networks in Western Europe. Agde is connected by high-speed or TGV (*train à grand vitesse*) train services from Paris, which makes travelling to Cap d'Agde by train an attractive and often quicker alternative to driving. From the United Kingdom, Eurostar trains speed between London and Paris via the Channel Tunnel in three hours, and services operated by Thalys cover the distance between Brussels and Paris in about half this time. The trip from Paris to Agde takes a little over four hours, which means that if you are coming from London, the total journey time including connections is eight or nine hours. Driving from the French Channel ports to Cap d'Agde takes at least 13 hours, and a few more to travel from London to France.

A one-way ticket on the TGV from Paris to Agde costs from 70 euro depending on when you travel. To find out more about fares and to make reservations, visit the SNCF (Société Nationale des Chemins de Fer) website, www.sncf.fr.

Once in Cap d'Agde, the most convenient place to make enquiries about train travel is at the friendly SNCF office near the port in the clothed part of town (see the map on page 168). Opening hours are: Mon.–Sat. 10.00–13.00 and 15.00–19.00 from June 17 to July 6 and September 1 to 7; and 09.30–13.00 and 14.30–19.00 from July 8 to August 31.

Once you have arrived at the train station in Agde, you still have a little work to do to get to the nudist resort. A bus (#273) picks up passengers in front of the train station and does a loop of Cap d'Agde, passing the main accommodations in the clothed part of town before stopping at the entrance to the nudist resort. The bus then returns directly to the train station. Although the bus takes 45 minutes to travel from the train station to the nudist resort, travelling the opposite direction only takes 15 minutes. About 10 buses a day run the route Mondays to Saturdays; expect considerably fewer on Sundays and public holidays. The flat fare is around 2 euro and change (within reason) is given.

Alternatively, you can take a taxi. The fare from the SNCF station should be 20 to 25 euro, and drivers are accustomed to going to the nudist resort—so don't be shy.

Warming up in Paris

Stopping in Paris en route to Cap d'Agde will be a tempting proposition for libertines, whether they are arriving in France by air or travelling down from northern Europe and looking for somewhere to break their journey. This stopover is not a must because the French capital is inundated with nudist beaches, but rather because Paris, as well as being the most romantic city in the world, is also one of the naughtiest. This dual personality means that you can walk hand-in-hand down the Champs-Elysée with your beloved, enjoy a picnic by the Seine, dinner at a cosy restaurant in Montmartre, then pass a wild night of dancing and debauchery at one of the nearly 50 sex clubs in the Paris area.

And finding these clubs is not a question of making sleazy enquires of your taxi driver; clubs are openly advertised in local magazines and newspapers. Indeed, for Parisians of all ages, going to a club where you have the option of wearing sexy and revealing clothes, groping on the dance floor, and taking activities further without having to ask the awkward 'your place or mine' question has become a legitimate alternative to going to a 'normal' disco where aggressive, drunken behaviour makes much of the above rather less appealing.

The style and format of the Parisian clubs is much the same as in Cap d'Agde (for more on what to expect in these types of places, see *Carnal Clubbing* on page 95), the main difference being that in Paris the choice is larger and, consequently, you must shop around for the club that is right for you. Also note that, while in Cap d'Agde you can usually wear ultra-casual attire, in Paris dress codes are strictly enforced: which means no jeans and trainers (gym shoes) for the men and no trousers for the women.

When Charles Darwin was studying finches on the Galápagos Islands about 170 years ago, he noticed that, of the birds living on the more arid land, the ones with beaks better suited for eating cactus found more food. As a result, they were in a better condition to mate—and therefore survive. If swingers clubs had existed in 19th-century Paris (and who's to say they didn't?), Darwin might have saved himself a lengthy voyage before coming up with the theory of natural selection. For in certain clubs, only those with the finest beaks get to eat the cactus.

At places such as **Les Chandelles** and **Le Cléopâtre,** for instance, you and your partner (couples only here) will be scrutinised heavily at the door before being allowed in to mingle with the show biz personalities, sports stars, and beautiful people who congregate at these exclusive addresses.

Don't be offended if you are refused entry, and head instead to **L'Overside, Deux Plus Deux,** or **Chris et Manu,** three of the capital's other busy and less fussy clubs, where you'll find plenty of more down-to-earth playmates. On two nights a week (Wednesdays and Sundays), L'Overside opens its doors to single men; otherwise, the afternoon gang-bangs at the venerable **La Cheminée** are always popular.

Being France, sex and food are never too far apart, and at **Chez Sorlut** couples can eat at a restaurant where the main dish is served under the table. Fetishists and BDSM enthusiasts also are not forgotten, with **Le Bar-Bar** the notable place to visit. A book in itself could be written about the alternative lifestyle in Paris. This section is designed only to make you aware of the possibilities of fun in the city beyond the terminal building at Charles de Gaulle Airport.

A listing of the sexy nightlife on offer in Paris is published in *Pariscope*, a weekly magazine containing information on what to do in the capital. Alternatively, turn to *Quick Reference* on page 183 for the contact details of the clubs mentioned in this section. Always call the club before you visit to check that what you have read is still valid.

Stepping across the threshold

Congratulations! You have spat in the face of convention and made the decision to visit Cap d'Agde. You have packed wisely for your trip, and shopped around for the best deal to get you here. Now, after a long journey (perhaps with a pit stop in Paris), you stand at the entrance to the resort, itching to peel off your sweaty clothes and kick back on a terrace with a pastis and a bowl of olives. The last thing that you need at this point is bureaucracy—but that irritation is exactly what you find.

Unless pre-arranged by your tour operator, you must purchase a card to enter the nudist resort. These cards vary in price depending on how long you intend to stay and whether you are entering on foot or by car. Current tariffs are:

Foot access

Daily: 2,80 euro	Two weeks: 17 euro
Two days: 5,60 euro	Three weeks: 26 euro
Three days: 8,40 euro	Four weeks: 33,50 euro
One week: 11 euro	Whole season: 55 euro

Car access

Daily: 9 euro	Two weeks: 52 euro
Two days: 18 euro	Three weeks: 60 euro
Three days: 27 euro	Four weeks: 70 euro
One week: 37 euro	Whole season: 110 euro

Note that cards valid for less than one week will not work after 20.00. This time is also when the *Bureau d'Accueil* (Welcome Office) closes for the day, so arrive before then to purchase your card. Otherwise, entering the resort town depends on your ability to convince the security guard of your credentials. Showing a confirmed reservation at the campsite, hotel, or with one of the agencies renting apartments helps.

Once in, you need not buy a card for the duration of your stay if you intend to spend the entire time within the confines

42

of the resort; cards are only required by those wishing to move freely between the nudist community and the clothed world.

Tightwads will be pleased to know you can enter the resort without having to pay for a card: simply walk to the nudist beach from Marseillan Beach (see the map on page 44). Although this walk is okay during daylight hours, walking on the sand is not recommended at night when you are all dressed up and wearing mile-high stiletto heels. Quite apart from this difficulty, security on the beach at night is questionable.

Orientation and acclimatisation

Once inside, you might wonder why Cap d'Agde has been referred to as a 'resort' throughout this book. Indeed, had there not been a proper town, also called Cap d'Agde, nearby, the nudist resort would surely justify a grander description. Names aside, however, you should not think of Cap d'Agde as a resort like those found in, say, the Caribbean: a couple of hundred rooms and a swimming pool around a stretch of sandy beach. For the naked part of Cap d'Agde *is* a town— albeit a small one—and you will need to appreciate this fact when finding your bearings.

The lay of the land

The *quartier naturiste* of Cap d'Agde extends east from Port Ambonne to Marseillan Beach and northwest from the Mediterranean Sea to the marshy land known as the Réserve Naturelle du Bagnas (Bagnas Natural Reserve).

Free maps of the resort are available at the Welcome Office at the entrance and, along with the map in this guide, should be more than sufficient to help you find your way around. Everything is accessible on foot. The longest walk— from Hotel Eve to the gay beach, for example—will not take more than 25 minutes.

The nudist beach or *plage naturiste* is about 2km long. No official distinction is made between the different parts of this beach, although in reality it is three beaches in one. What has been described in this book as the 'family beach' extends from

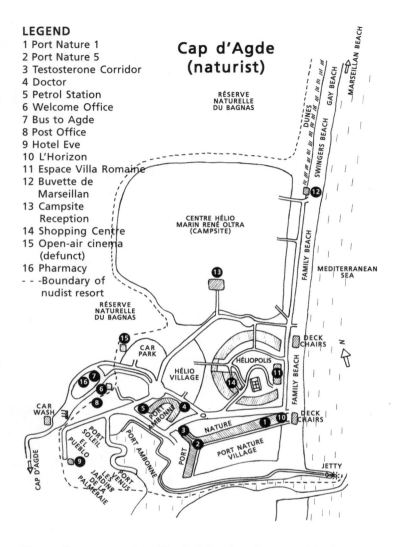

LEGEND

1 Port Nature 1
2 Port Nature 5
3 Testosterone Corridor
4 Doctor
5 Petrol Station
6 Welcome Office
7 Bus to Agde
8 Post Office
9 Hotel Eve
10 L'Horizon
11 Espace Villa Romaine
12 Buvette de Marseillan
13 Campsite Reception
14 Shopping Centre
15 Open-air cinema (defunct)
16 Pharmacy
- - -Boundary of nudist resort

Cap d'Agde (naturist)

RÉSERVE NATURELLE DU BAGNAS

MARSEILLAN BEACH

DUNES

GAY BEACH

SWINGERS BEACH

CENTRE HÉLIO MARIN RENÉ OLTRA (CAMPSITE)

FAMILY BEACH

MEDITERRANEAN SEA

RÉSERVE NATURELLE DU BAGNAS

CAR PARK

DECK CHAIRS

HÉLIO VILLAGE

HÉLIOPOLIS

FAMILY BEACH

N

CAR WASH

PORT SOLEIL

EL PUEBLO

PORT AMBONNE

PORT AMBONNE

PORT LES VENUS

JARDINS DE LA PALMERAIE

PORT AMBONNE

PORT NATURE

PORT NATURE VILLAGE

DECK CHAIRS

CAP D'AGDE

JETTY

The nudist resort at Cap d'Agde is bordered on two sides by water—the Mediterranean and a port. The naturist beach is about 2km long.

the jetty to more or less the end of the campsite, marked by a restaurant called the Buvette de Marseillan. From here, the swingers beach occupies the next 300m or so of sand, after which the gay beach continues to the point where the naturist section ends and the clothed Marseillan Beach begins. The dunes line the back of the swingers and gay beach.

The family beach is home to all types: families with children of all ages, pure naturists, libertines not interested in watching public displays of sex, resort workers on their days off, and people who can't be bothered to walk too far from their accommodation to find a place to sunbathe. The swingers beach is a meeting place for heterosexual exhibitionists, voyeurs, and swingers looking to meet other swingers. The gay beach is the homosexual version of the swingers beach.

The 'town' part of the resort can be split into four sections, each with its own accommodation, shops, and restaurants. Port Ambonne is opposite the port bearing the same name; Port Soleil and other apartment complexes (including Hotel Eve) are clustered round the western edge of the port; Port Nature stretches from the eastern edge of the port to the beach; and Héliopolis, a near circular building, occupies the geographical centre of the resort. The campsite is a vast area of more or less green space that extends from Héliopolis to the northeastern perimeters of the resort.

In this guide, certain place names crop up again and again when describing life in the resort. Port Nature, for example, is not just apartments; it also is the address of many of the Cap's businesses, concentrated at either Port Nature 1 (the beach end of Port Nature) or Port Nature 5 (also known as 'Le Noyau'—which is about 200m inland).

More shops, restaurants, and bars line a corridor that links Port Nature 5 and Port Ambonne. In the absence of any formal name for this part of the resort, it has been dubbed '**Testosterone Corridor**' in this book in recognition of its raunchy bars, sexy boutiques, and heaving mass of debauched humanity during high season. Note, however, that if you ask someone to direct you to Testosterone Corridor, you will be met with blank looks.

Getting used to being naked

Nudity is permitted absolutely everywhere within the boundaries of the resort, and this fact, rather than the actual lay of the land, will present the greatest challenge when trying to adapt to your new surroundings. Here are some tips to acclimatise to living in a naked town:

- First-timers should consider planning their arrival at around dusk. People start to cover up at this time and rarely do you see naked bodies at night, thus giving you precious time to become accustomed to the idea of being naked in this place. But erecting a tent in darkness is complicated, so campers should plan accordingly.

- Unless you feel comfortable and secure about your nakedness, rushing to the shops in the nude will win you points for bravery, but also a face as red as your sunburnt buttocks when you discover that you are the only naked person in a supermarket full of well-dressed shoppers, all of whom you are convinced are staring at you (which they are almost certainly not). Nothing will put you off the whole nudism thing like a baptism of fire such as this. Ease yourself into nudity on the beach before deciding what else you want to do.

- The comfortable and confident naturists referred to above should nevertheless remember to bring something in which to put their change when shopping. The human body only offers so many storage spaces, and the euro coins are not the smallest and lightest in the world.

- Those with delicate dispositions might prefer the self-catering option if naked diners with bodies like Jabba the Hutt are liable to put them off their food.

- Just because you *can* be naked anywhere and at any time does not necessarily mean that you *should*. Certain activities, such as the morning aerobics sessions at the campsite and similar activities involving the spreading of legs and much jigging about, usually are performed wearing some item of clothing.

- Most people adapt quickly to being naked and carrying out their daily activities in the nude. You must remember, however, to put something on when you leave the resort. France might be an open-minded country, but nudity outside the *quartier naturiste* is still an arrestable offence. When you walk too far on the beach and realise that everyone is clothed, you also had best turn around.

Whether this trip is your first naked holiday or your hundredth, two things are for sure: you will quickly realise that, in the beauty stakes, someone is always worse off than yourself, and, in any case, no one gives a rat's arse about your physical imperfections. One of the main attractions for people who practice naturism is its ability to be the greatest of levellers.

Colin from London (U.K.), who, along with his wife Melanie, is a nudist novice, expected everyone to be top models and action men. 'But they're not. Coming here makes you realise that nobody's perfect. If you're not a few pounds overweight, you've got skinny legs; and if you've got a fat bum, you've probably also got nice—'

'Eyes.'

'Yeah, that's right, Mel! Going on a naturist holiday is like taking a reality pill—and it's done wonders for my confidence.'

Somewhat ironically, even in a nudist resort such as Cap d'Agde where sex plays an important role, you will probably end up being stared at less than you would on a conventional, clothed beach. Cap d'Agde also has a better reputation than other nudist resorts of a similar style for allowing people to merge unnoticed into the crowd.

'Unlike some other sexy nudist venues such as Hedonism II in Jamaica and Paradise Lakes in Tampa, Florida, Cap d'Agde doesn't make me feel as though I have to hold my stomach in all day,' says Chris from Chicago (USA), who has visited the Cap three times.

The vastness of the resort compared with other naturist centres also could help overcome shyness or other concerns preventing you from acclimatising to the idea of being naked. 'Because of the size of the complex you see new people all the time. You're quite anonymous and that's what we prefer,' say Yvon and Max from Amsterdam (Holland).

Even naturists need a roof over their heads

Accommodations in Cap d'Agde are of mediocre quality and overpriced. Americans don't find the rates appalling, but they do tend to question the value for money when they have been booked into an apartment that has not been redecorated in 35 years. Europeans find the situation easier to cope with than the more demanding North American visitors such as Ron from Florida who describes his two weeks in the Cap as 'rustic living'. Much of the accommodation is rough around the edges and in need of serious sprucing up. But the selection is enormous, and you can find comfortable and reasonably priced digs if you know where to look.

Cap d'Agde offers three types of accommodation: self-catering apartments, hotel rooms, and camping. Wherever you choose to stay, you must fork out a visitors tax (added to your bill), which varies in amount depending on where you are staying—for example, campers pay 0,17 euro a day and guests at Hotel Eve pay 0,82 euro.

The apartments

The vast majority of accommodation in Cap d'Agde is apartments. These rentals can either be in multistoried

Avoiding Port Nature is difficult. The L-shaped complex stretching from the eastern edge of the port to the beach is home to numerous apartments, two swimming pools, several of the resort's finest restaurants and boutiques, and the notorious nightlife along Testosterone Corridor.

apartment complexes, such as the circular Héliopolis, the L-shaped Port Nature, and the crescent-shaped Port Ambonne, or semi-detached villas in shady, traffic-free parts of the resort called 'villages'. Although for the most part rented by agencies, almost all of the apartments in Cap d'Agde are privately owned—and often used by the owners when not being rented out. The result is that every apartment has its own character, depending on the taste of its owner. And although sometimes as kitsch as a 1970s porn movie (which for some people may be a definite plus), the furnishings almost always include the following:

- A bed of some description and, in the slightly larger apartments, bunk beds for extra people. (Linen also is provided and changed once a week.)
- A table and chairs for eating
- A kitchen equipped with cutlery and cooking utensils
- A bathroom
- Some closet space

Most places have some form of outdoor space, be it a balcony, terrace, or small garden (as is the case with many of the villas). Some of the more luxurious places include crea-

Port Ambonne, the first brick construction in Cap d'Agde, overlooks the eponymous port, and remains one of the resort's focal points for shopping, leisure activities, and acommodations.

ture comforts such as televisions (French channels only), sofas and armchairs, microwave ovens, dishwashers, and private garages. Note, however, that air conditioning is almost unheard of; for that you'll need to check into the hotel (see *Hotel Eve* on page 51).

American visitors should remember that the floor system in France is different from the United States. The first floor is really the second floor—which can make a big difference if you book a room on the third floor and have to walk up three flights of stairs. Not all of the apartment complexes have lifts (elevators). If a lift matters, enquire about one when making your reservation.

Unlike at a hotel, you are expected to leave the apartment as you found it. You must wash the dishes and clean the bathroom, although you are not expected to launder the sheets. Failure to comply could result in money being taken from your deposit. Most agencies only allow you to check in on a Saturday and require a minimum seven-night stay (shorter stays are usually possible in low season or with certain agencies. Rental is by the apartment and not per person, so you can save money by sharing with others.

When making a reservation, a deposit of around 25% of the total bill is required. A further deposit of usually not less than 150 euro is payable on arrival to cover breakages and the like. This money can be in the form of a cheque (which is not cashed) or a credit card deposit, and it is returned a week or two after you have left, assuming no problems are found with the apartment.

Generalising about the cost of renting apartments in Cap d'Agde is difficult. Much depends on factors such as size, position, and especially the time of the year. The following, however, is a rough guide to prices for seven nights:

Studios (sleeping two): 170–520 euro

Studios (sleeping four): 210–665 euro

Two-room apartments (sleeping up to six): 290–700 euro

Villas (sleeping up to eight): 330–1,500 euro

The first brick construction in Cap d'Agde was Port Ambonne; Port Nature and Héliopolis followed soon after. These three apartment complexes are the most dated—and the cheapest. Next to Port Nature and Héliopolis are two 'villages', where you can find semi-detached villas (or townhouses) with private patios or gardens. The newer developments such as Port Venus, Port Soleil, and the larger, more sumptuous villas at El Pueblo and Les Jardins de la Palmeraie are clustered round the western edge of Port Ambonne.

For a complete list of agencies renting apartments in Cap d'Agde, see *Quick Reference* on page 183. Most have offices at the entrance. If finding vacancies in the nudist resort itself is proving difficult, you could stay in one of the many accommodations in the clothed part of Cap d'Agde and make daily visits to the naked part of town. Check **www.capdagde.com** for the possibilities. Another way of finding a place to stay, but only once you have arrived at the resort, is to check the notice boards at the supermarkets and commercial centres. Sometimes private owners advertise their properties here rather than through an agency.

Hotel Eve
Impasse Saissan (04 67 26 71 70; www.hoteleve.com)

That the nudist resort only has one hotel remains a source of mystery. Less puzzling, however, is the fact that it, like much of the other accommodation in the Cap, is nothing more than average. Hotel Eve, located on the western edge of the resort, makes much of its three-star status. Its four-star prices are no doubt the result of its lack of competition.

The 48 rooms are not too bad. All are en suite, have satellite TV, telephone, mini-bar, and safe, and 32 of them are air-conditioned. The hotel also has a sauna, a rooftop sun terrace, and a small swimming pool that is guaranteed to be a lot quieter than the public pools around the resort. Single rooms with no air conditioning range from 55 euro a night in low season to 88 euro in high season, and double rooms cost 66 to 100 euro a night. Add a further 8 euro for air conditioning; and another 8 euro for a buffet breakfast.

The campsite

Avenue des Néréides (04 67 01 06 36; www.chm-reneoltra.com)

If the naked part of Cap d'Agde consisted of no more than the Centre Hélio Marin René Oltra—as it did in the beginning—it would be an impressive naturist centre. For this vast campsite of more than 2,500 sites, occupying a large

Hotel Eve is the *quartier naturiste's* only hotel, and you can book for less than one week. It is one of the few accommodations in the nudist resort with some air conditioning, which isn't always needed, but occasionally refreshing. PHOTO: Mark Ashworth

chunk of the eastern part of the *quartier naturiste*, is truly a resort within a resort.

Decidedly more naturist-friendly than anywhere else in Cap d'Agde, the campsite offers not only a place to lay your head but also a range of activities for the whole family. Picture screaming kids, annoying announcements at the crack of dawn about the fun-filled day in store for happy campers, foam discos, and ballroom dancing to be halfway to understanding what the campsite is all about.

Renate from Eindhoven (Holland), one of the smiling faces at the campsite's reception desk, provides context: 'I think that Cap d'Agde is a place for everybody. The village [resort] is separated in two: one for the people looking for freedom, sex, extreme art (in their way of dressing), and new experi-

52

ences in their relationships; and the other for the naturist who wants to be free in the nature and find friends who enjoy the same lifestyle—nothing to do with sex, just the freedom to be naked. The first part you find in the village and the second in the camping. I think that the control is good enough to let people make the choice and not be confronted by the other group if they don't want to be.'

The campsite remains the best place in the whole resort to avoid the sexual overtones present elsewhere—well, almost. What gives the place its edge has been the management's inability to keep out the libertines. Okay, so stockings and suspenders (garters) and campfires are not natural bedfellows, but they sure give the campsite a devilish alter ego which, while kept in check by its angelic side, is nevertheless bubbling beneath the respectable surface. The libertines seem to give scant regard to the campsite's attempts to keep the place wholesome, the latest of which has been to ban body piercings. Sexy games continue to be played clandestinely despite the constant presence of the internal security personnel, who wear bright orange T-shirts (see Chapter 4 about libertines on page 79).

You don't have to have a tent, caravan, or RV to stay at the campsite. Mobile homes and chalets (the difference between the two is hard to say) sleeping from two to six people and with facilities similar to the apartments in the resort (including private bathrooms) are available for those who have neither the equipment nor the inclination to camp. Since there are only a relatively few of these, you should reserve in advance.

A modest patch of ground about half the size of a tennis court awaits the other campers. Some who lease this land on a yearly basis have managed to make their sites look quite homey by planting small gardens, building fences, and putting up 'Home Sweet Home' or 'Chien méchant' (bad dog) signs depending on whether they want to attract or deter visitors. Most campers, though, park their caravans or pitch their tents and make the best of what they have.

Ablution blocks with toilets, showers, and basins for washing clothes and dishes are located strategically around the grounds, and your site is never too far from one. Showers are often only lukewarm and forbidden for a few hours in the afternoon (for cleaning) and after 23.00. Safety deposit boxes at reception can be rented by the day (3

Renate and Isa enjoy a rare moment of relaxation in the usually hectic reception of the C.H.M. René Oltra campsite.

euro) or by the week (7 euro), but they can only be accessed during reception opening hours. The sites are laid out in rows and numbered alphabetically. Allée Mer is closest to the beach (about 50m) followed by Allée Plage, Allée Dune, Allée A, Allée B, Allée C, all the way up to Allée O.

In keeping with its efforts to remain as close to the naturist (as opposed to the libertine) ideal as possible, everyone staying at the campsite is required to be a member of the Fédération Française de Naturisme. This membership costs 20 euro and is valid for one year. After that, daily rates for the various accommodations on offer are as follows:

Tent, caravan, or RV site (for two people and a car): 16,30–29,50 euro

Tent, caravan, or RV site (for four people and a car):

25,30–29,50 euro

    Chalet (sleeping two people): 46–73 euro

    Mobile home (sleeping four to six people): 46–77 euro

    Chalet (sleeping six people): 70–102 euro

A deposit of 25% of the total bill is required when you make a reservation, plus a non-refundable reservation fee of 23 euro. Just turning up in the hope of getting a site is possible most of the time except for the first two weeks in August. Even then, you might find a place for a day or two in between bookings. For the mobile homes and chalets, a seven-night minimum stay is required during high season.

The type of accommodation for you?
The spendthrift

The cheapest daily accommodation is at the campsite. You could also save money by inviting 10 of your friends to share your apartment. Otherwise, cheap deals such as 14 nights for the price of 10 are offered by the rental agencies at the beginning and end of the season (usually before mid-June and after the end of August). The really budget conscious might consider sleeping in their cars or renting a garage instead of an apartment and living there.

The first-class traveller

Go to Saint-Tropez.

The party animal

You would be a little naïve to come to the Cap and think that you could host wild swingers parties in your one-man tent. Indeed, inviting anyone back to such rudimentary digs is a risky policy if you want to have your wicked way with them. In fact, stay away from the campsite altogether to avoid the risk of offending the many families and serious naturists. What potential party organisers need is an apartment, the bigger the better, and preferably with two separate rooms: one for serving the nibbles, the other for being nibbled. A studio is fine for threesomes and foursomes.

The performer

Every performer needs a stage, and in Cap d'Agde stages

come in the form of apartment terraces. Those interested in putting on peep shows for interested passers-by should decide whether they want to give the voyeurs a seat in the front row or the gallery. The terraces in Port Nature and Hélio Village are both good for the former since they can be accessed from public footpaths. The balconies at Héliopolis put a little more distance between you and your audience. Avoiding being rumbled by the security guards (see *Les Gendarmes du Cap* on page 67) spices up what many already find to be an exhilarating activity.

The romantic

Some guests use their terraces and balconies to do nothing more than enjoy the sunset and other fine views (rather than be enjoyed *as* the fine view). The higher apartments in Héliopolis C, D, and E, and Port Nature 6, 7, and 8 are all places from where you can watch the sunset. The best apartments for sea views are in Port Nature 1 and Héliopolis O, AB, F, G, and H, and the residences at Port Vénus overlook the reasonably picturesque Port Ambonne.

The dirty weekender

Given that most agencies renting apartments require a seven-night minimum stay during high season, those coming to the Cap for a dirty weekend are best off booking into Hotel Eve. The alternative would be to take a place at the campsite, although staying in an air-conditioned room with clean sheets and a sturdy bed as opposed to a tent could mean the difference between spending a dirty weekend and just spending the weekend dirty.

The family

The campsite is the place for kids. Not only does it offer the adventure of camping, but it also provides activities for the youngsters during the day and at night.

The pure naturist

Once again, the campsite is the place to be. This location, after all, is where it all began, and the campsite still tries to attract naturists rather than libertines. Apartments also are an option, although you have no control over neighbours who may insist on bumping and grinding well into the early hours. But not all of the apartments are riddled with passionate nighttime revelry.

The beauty sleeper

Avoid the apartments in Port Nature above the Melrose and other bars on Testosterone Corridor (Port Nature 6, 7, and 8). The music is turned down at midnight, but this area is still the noisiest in the resort.

The RV owner

The RV owner will already have accommodations. Officially you are supposed to park RVs in the campsite, but in the height of summer there will probably be no room. Even if there is room, you could be too cheap to fork out for a site. You will not be alone. During August, ad hoc RV villages spring up in the car parks and at the entrance to the resort. According to the municipal police who address such matters, you are apparently allowed to park in any one place for 48 hours. So, provided you don't become too attached to a particular spot, you should have no problems with the law.

Degustation

Cap d'Agde might be in France, the home of fine cooking, but so is Paris, and you don't see naked people walking round the Louvre on a Sunday afternoon. Swimming against the flow as always, Cap d'Agde lacks the consistently fine dining opportunities found elsewhere in the country. Some of the many restaurants in the resort have pretensions of grandeur, but only a few serve food of the quality to justify the hefty price tag. Of course when you can eat at a restaurant with just a napkin to prevent errant strands of spaghetti catching in your pubes, maybe the standard of the food does not need to be all that high. This philosophy seems reflected by too many restaurateurs in the Cap, where the pleasures of eating out are often to be found more in the company you keep and the colourful characters constantly passing by than the food itself.

All the above is what a French or an Italian reviewer might say about the restaurants in Cap d'Agde. However, for those coming from the pariah states of the culinary world (you know who you are), the choice and quality of the eateries will not be so much of an issue as what all the fancy dishes actually *are*. Unfussy eaters will happily wolf down what the resort has to offer by way of sustenance, and in this sense Cap d'Agde is as good a place as any to find a decent meal.

'Unlike small naturist resorts, Cap d'Agde, being a town, has a wide range of places to eat from pizzerias to French gourmet restaurants,' say Ann and David from Cap d'Agde. The resort offers more than 40 eateries to choose from. Restaurants are concentrated in the commercial centres of Port Nature, Port Ambonne, and Héliopolis. A few more can be found on the beach, at Port Soleil, and the entrance to the resort (where clothing is required). Most restaurants are open mid-May to mid-September, and some only serve dinner.

Visitors from the United States who enjoy big mugs of coffee that are refilled repeatedly will be disappointed. The coffee is served in relatively small cups—and refilled only upon request and at an additional cost. At least the quality of the coffee is generally good.

Tap water can be requested for free and it tastes fine, but most people order bottled water—*sans gaz* or *l'eau plat* is still water, *avec gaz* is carbonated.

Chic and expensive—but are they worth it?

The owners of the rival swingers clubs in the resort, Le Juls and Le Glamour, also run two restaurants that are considered to be among the best places to eat. **Brasserie Le Bistro** (04 67 26 39 38) in Port Nature 5 opposite its sister establishment, Le Juls, is the less pretentious of the two. The large terrace on one of the resort's busiest traffic-free thoroughfares is excellent for people-watching, especially at night when the flow of revellers from the apartments of Port Nature to the boutiques and bars along Testosterone Corridor is almost constant.

The food, meanwhile, is *nouvelle cuisine*: sparrow-like portions of artistically presented Provençal meat and seafood dishes. Okay if you don't want to be bloated for the night of physical exertion that lies ahead; not substantial enough to line your stomach in preparation for a heavy drinking session.

Expect slightly more from the menu-only (fixed price) meals at **Restaurant Villa Romaine** (04 67 01 38 42), part of the Espace Villa Romaine (which includes Le Glamour), but don't expect to be allowed entrance if you are wearing shorts and a T-shirt. Naked diners, meanwhile, will be informed with the politeness for which the Villa Romaine is so famous to get stuffed. A section of the Cap's population feels at home in such affected surroundings, and Villa Romaine is probably the place to go on your date with the fashion model you met on the beach earlier in the afternoon.

The whiter-than-white tablecloths, sparkling cutlery, and intimate lighting are not devoid of class, the diners are undoubtedly rather good looking, the *fois gras* and oyster starters are luxurious, but something about the Villa Romaine does not sit well with the Cap d'Agde mentality. The restaurant is more Paris or Los Angeles than open-minded, easy-going nudist resort in the south of France. The cheapest menus, which include a starter, main course, dessert, and coffee, start at 27 euro.

Along with the Bistro-versus-Villa Romaine matchup, another struggle exists—this time for seafood supremacy—between two restaurants with interwoven pasts. Fifteen years ago, Poissonnerie Chez Maxime used to be *the* restaurant in Cap d'Agde, with its three servings a day and three-day waiting lists for a table. Standards slipped slightly when the restaurant moved from its Port Ambonne site to larger premises at the entrance to the resort, although it continues to be extremely popular. Nowadays it's known simply as La Poissonnerie.

Another seafood restaurant, confusingly called Poissonnerie Chez Maxime, has opened in the place previously occupied by the original Poissonnerie Chez Maxime and has become La Poissonerie's main competition. Instead of trying to remember who's who, just bear in mind that both of these restaurants serve seafood—and only seafood. Platters laden with crabs, mussels, oysters, shrimps, and lobster start at 15 euro and can go up to as much as 90 euro for two people.

La Poissonerie (04 67 26 25 66), at the entrance to the nudist resort (if you weren't paying attention earlier), continues to set the standard. The sprawling dining room is always buzzing with activity as waiters in black bow ties deliver various crustacea to the many tables inside and on the grass outside.

Poissonnerie Chez Maxime (04 67 26 03 71) is a lot smaller and more sedate in comparison. You can eat in its dining room tucked away in a quiet corner of Port Ambonne or on the terrace by the swimming pool, a location shared by a few other bars and restaurants.

La Grange Gourmande (04 67 01 57 74) deserves special mention among these fancy eateries as the Cap's most obviously gay-friendly restaurant. At 15 euro and up for a main dish, this restaurant is not the cheapest place in town, but the food is well prepared and French in style.

Casa Nueva (04 67 26 08 15), next to the Melrose Café on Testosterone Corridor, is another trendy place to eat. The main advantages here are that meals are served until late in the evening (usually around 01.00) and the choice, though limited, is often quite imaginative. Given that the restaurant often plays host to public whipping sessions and other forms of exotic entertainment, appropriately the food on offer is more *cuisses de grenouilles aux pistaches* than sausage and chips (French fries). At 12,50 euro, the dishes are not bad value either.

A restaurant with a view

The grassy terrace at **L'Horizon** (04 67 26 00 32), a large restaurant in Port Nature 1 overlooking the sea, is a

Cap d'Agde landmark, and over the years some famous naked buttocks (such as those of photographer David Hamilton, who owned an apartment in the Cap for 20 years) have sat on its plastic chairs and enjoyed the stellar sea and beach views. On sunny days the parasols go up—and in any case there is enough shade provided by the surrounding trees to keep you from getting too sticky. The food is unspectacular and the service brusque, although the choice on the menu is good. Main dishes start at around 11 euro.

The restaurants next to L'Horizon, also with terraces overlooking the beach, are similar in style—albeit slightly smaller and less imposing. Choose from **Le Mississippi** (04 67 01 51 19), immediately next to L'Horizon, or **Le Calypso** (04 67 26 85 13), a little further towards the jetty. All these terraces require varying degrees of neck craning to view the sunset. Better, perhaps, to install yourself at one of the tables on the west-facing terrace at **Le Baskin** (04 67 26 40 71) in Port Nature 1 opposite the swimming pool, and order one of the ice creams or cocktails for which the place is renowned.

Somewhat removed from all the above establishments, about a kilometre further down the beach, is the **Buvette de Marseillan** (04 67 94 44 01), a place referred to quite often in this guide because it marks the unofficial end of the family beach and the beginning of the area frequented by libertines. This fact alone makes the Buvette an interesting place to go for a sundowner if you missed the opportunity to hook up with people during the day on the beach. The restaurant is located at the last point at which you can access the nudist beach from the resort, and since most of the people who use this entrance are heading for the swingers or gay beach, the terrace at the Buvette is the prime location for checking out the talent. The menu has good, honest, and reasonably priced food served by friendly staff until around 22.00. A good place to eat lunch (especially the mussels), rehydrate, and enjoy the view.

The foreign touch

Although hardly a gastronomic treat for lovers of foreign cuisine, Cap d'Agde does have several places where you can find slightly more exotic food. The sign of **Le Rajasthan** (04 67 26 47 44) in Port Soleil is visible from the entrance to the resort and is a comforting sight for the many foreign visitors—particularly from the United Kingdom—who have been brought up on Indian food (Indians themselves are not numerous in the Cap). Unfortunately, as is so often the case at such restaurants in France, what should be spicy, fiery dishes have been tempered so as not to offend delicate French palates. The result is food with Indian names, but only the slightest hint of an Indian flavour. Connoisseurs will be disappointed, especially since the meals here are not cheap.

The situation is more encouraging for sushi-lovers, with the opening of **Yumi's** (06 99 08 18 84) in Port Nature 1. This small Japanese restaurant of only about four or five tables has six national dishes for 7,70 euro each and sushi meals for 6,90 euro (five pieces) or 10 euro (10 pieces). Elsewhere in the resort, you can find Creole food at **La Case Creole** (04 67 00 12 26) in Héliopolis and average Tex-Mex offerings at **Viva Mexico** (04 67 00 02 31) on Testosterone Corridor, where the service and ambiance are as sterile as the opportunities for people-watching are fruitful.

Something cheap and fast

You will rarely have a problem finding something cheap and fast in Cap d'Agde, which applies for the food as well. Functional, family restaurants where you can quite easily find a fix of pasta or chicken and chips for under 10 euro abound in the resort. Good examples include: **Le Ghymnos** (04 67 26 06 09) in Héliopolis, one of the few restaurants to remain open after the end of the season, where the wood-oven churns out reasonably priced pizzas and grilled meat dishes; **Oasis Tropical** (04 67 26 68 08) in Port Nature 1 near the beach, where a fixed *menu du jour* can be had for just over 10 euro; and **La Dégustation** in Port Nature 5, where you are invited to eat as many *moules frites* (mussels and chips) as you can for only 9 euro.

In the absence of McDonald's and other recognisable chains (for them, you'll have to venture into Agde), fast food in the nudist resort basically boils down to several holes-in-the-wall selling pizzas, kebabs, and various greasy delicacies served with chips. The pick of the bunch—by virtue of the two wooden benches at which you can eat your food if you don't feel like taking it back to your lodgings—is **Pizza Flora** (04 67 26 53 56) in Port Ambonne. Along with the pizzas, you can order *merguez* (spicy sausage) and chips and salads. Another good place for pizza, this time in Port Nature 1, is **Pizza Mania** (04 67 01 34 34), which has free delivery. The nearby **La Canne à Sucre** (06 03 86 35 19) specialises in kebabs and various other sandwiches, and is open until 02.00.

Where to put your change: Shopping naked

The uniqueness of Cap d'Agde is that, in addition to the accommodation and restaurants that you would expect to find at nudist resorts the world over, the *quartier naturiste* quarter has an infrastructure befitting a small town. Almost every Cap d'Agde photo album has shots of Barry doing the groceries—naked; Helen buying stamps for her postcards—naked; Fritz changing money at the bank—naked; and Claudia having her hair done—naked. You can find most of what you need for a vacation without ever leaving the resort. The following is a list of the shops and services that may be of use during your stay:

- **Supermarkets**—Five supermarkets are in the resort (two each in Port Ambonne and Port Nature and one in Héliopolis). Although none is particularly large, you should have no problem finding run-of-the-mill items such as eggs, milk, juice, pasta, toiletries, and the like. These supermarkets are generally open every day from late June to the end of August (at other times they will be open, but perhaps

Cap d'Agde differs from other nudist resorts because of the extent of the facilities available. Don't underestimate the mileage to be had at dinner parties back home from the story about when you went to the ATM to withdraw cash in nothing but your flip-flops. This activity may seem hilarious to your friends, but it's perfectly normal at the Cap.

not every day). They close for siesta around 13.00 to 16.00 and in the evenings at about 20.00 (the Vival supermarket in Port Ambonne is open until 23.00). On the outskirts of the town of Agde is a commercial centre with a couple of huge supermarkets selling everything from *fois gras* to economy toilet paper. The bus that links the nudist resort to the train station in Agde (see map on page 169) stops at the Hyper U supermarket.

- **Fruit and vegetables**—The supermarkets also have a selection of fruit and vegetables, but it's not as good as that found at the green grocers in Port Ambonne and Héliopolis.
- **Bakeries**—As you would expect in a French resort, a bakery is never too far away. Two are in Port Ambonne, and one each in Port Nature and Héliopolis. Those who have travelled a bit in France will have probably tasted better bread and pastries, though perhaps never in the

form of giant starchy penises or doughy breasts. The best place for naughty bread sculptures is the bakery opposite Le Pharaon in Port Ambonne.

- **Butchers**—Fresh meat and seafood, as well as a variety of other pre-prepared dishes such as paella, roast chicken, lasagne, and couscous, are available at butchers in Port Ambonne and Héliopolis. The best known of these is Boucherie Traiteur Raphaël, which opened in Héliopolis some 22 years ago.

- **Newsagents**—Known as *tabacs* in French, with a wide selection of (mostly French-language) magazines and newspapers, as well as cigarettes and sundry items for the beach (sunglasses, sun cream, lip balm, and the like).

- **Pharmacies**—The only place where you can get prescription drugs is at Pharmacie Nature (04 67 26 38 19) at the entrance to the nudist resort (so remember to put on some clothes). Summer opening hours are: Mon.–Sat. 09.30–20.00, Sun. 10.00–13.00 & 16.30–19.30.

- **Doctor**—There is a clinic in Port Ambonne (04 67 26 92 00). Visiting hours are: Mon.–Sat. 09.30–12.30 & 17.00–19.00, Sun. 10.00–12.30 & 17.00–19.00.

- **Bank**—A branch of Banque Dupuy de Parseval is in Port Ambonne and open Mon.–Fri. 09.00–12.00. You can change foreign currency and travellers' cheques here (the latter with a 5,75% commission). An **ATM** outside the bank accepts Visa, MasterCard but not American Express. Another ATM is opposite the filling station near the entrance gate and also takes all major cards except American Express.

- **Post office**—On entering the resort by foot, you will see the post office (La Poste) to your right. Opening hours are: Mon.–Fri. 09.30–12.00 & 14.00–16.00, Sat. 09.30–11.30. Collection times are: Mon.–Fri. 15.45, Sat 11.00.

- **Internet access**—Cap d'Agde went online in 2002 with the opening of a cyber café (which doesn't sell coffee) in Héliopolis. The front of the shop is full of video games, and the computers are in the back. The prices are some-what steep for surfing, but okay if you just want to check your e-mails from time to time. Fifteen minutes costs 3 euro, one hour is 10 euro, and five hours is 40 euro.

- **Hairdressers**—Getting your hair done (at least the hair on your head) may not be a top priority when in Cap d'Agde. Port Ambonne and Héliopolis host a couple of salons should you feel the urge.

- **Petrol station**—You can find a filling station opposite the entrance gate, where minor car repairs also are avail-able. Just outside the resort is a place to wash your car, 100m or so before you arrive at the entrance gate.

The above is not a comprehensive list of the shops and services available in the resort. You will also find gift shops, places to buy wine, a jeweller selling fancy Guy Laroche watches and jewellery by Fontenay and Bruce, as well as more offbeat offerings such as a shop specialising in saris, sarongs, and various trinkets and ornaments of an Indian and Oriental nature, and another doing a fine line in nauti-cal clothing and furniture. Who shops at such places re-mains a mystery—although should you need a sailor's uni-form, you won't have to go too far to find one.

For your eyes only: No photography

Photographing and video recording naked people is a sensitive issue, especially in France where personal privacy is serious business. As a general rule, only take pictures of people you know and who have given their consent to pose for your shots.

Some places, such as swingers clubs, is off-limits to cam-eras altogether, and at others, such as the swingers beach, you must be careful when brandishing your Nikon to record for posterity the sight of your partner skinny-dipping in the Mediterranean. Let the lens stray from its presumed target, and you risk being pounced on by several of the larger males on the beach, who will forcibly remove the camera and throw it or, if you're lucky, just the film into the sea. An exaggeration? Not always. Exactly this type of punishment has been meted out to shutter-happy offenders in past years, and the least you can expect is a verbal shaming in front of all of your would-be friends.

Such public humiliation has led to ways of concealing image-taking equipment of which James Bond would be proud. Take, for example, the gentleman who had installed a camera in his sunglasses and was operating the shutter with an attached wire hidden under his towel. Or the nature-lover who was pointing his camera at cute little seagulls bobbing up and down on the water but was actually seeing something quite different bobbing up and down at a 90° angle on the beach thanks to the aid of a two-way lens.

The best advice is to leave your camera at home. Otherwise, try to restrict your photo shoots to private gatherings with consenting subjects. Always ask before you include a stranger in your pictures. A **photo developing service** is at the Paris 16ème clothes boutique in Port Nature 1.

Les gendarmes du Cap

Forget the Cap's tired and overpriced facilities and its ambiguous personality, the hot topic of conversation under the parasols on the swingers beach for the past few years has been the increasing security presence around the resort, and particularly on the beach. Fans of dodgy French comedy from the 1960s and 70s may remember the series of films, *Les Gendarmes de Saint-Tropez*, in which hapless police spend their whole time trying to round up elusive nudists on a beach in Saint-Tropez.

Cap d'Agde has its own *gendarmes*, otherwise known as the CRS or Compagnies Républicaines de Sécurité (mobile units forming the general reserve of the national police force), who from the last weekend in June to the last weekend in August occupy a cabin next to the Buvette de Marseillan overlooking the swingers beach. In the past couple of years

the CRS have tended to linger well into the first and sometimes even the second week in September, a trend that looks
likely to continue in the foreseeable future. Every day between these dates they arrive promptly at 11.00, remaining
dutifully at their posts until around 21.00 or when everyone
has left. They pass their time monitoring the beach with
binoculars and patrolling the dunes on horseback.

Officially, their mission is to protect the birdlife and vegetation in the Réserve Naturelle du Bagnas (the expanse of
land behind the dunes), although cynics will quickly point out
that the daily trampling of hooves probably does more harm to
the natural habitat than any number of wandering naturists.
The CRS who patrol the swingers beach also are *maîtres
nageurs* (lifeguards), which could be another reason to justify
their presence. But their real purpose is to eradicate the sexual
shenanigans on the beach and in the dunes during the high
season, when children are all over the place and in need of
protection from impromptu sex shows.

Indeed, the situation was getting out of hand around the
mid-1990s. Until then, the exhibitionism and other touchy-
feelie stuff took place almost entirely in the relatively secluded
dunes, but then it started spilling out onto the beach for all to
see. The mayor of Agde decided that something needed to be
done, and the CRS were sent in to clean up the town.

And what a good job they have done: 'I was taking a pee in
the dunes,' says Neil from Chessington (U.K.), 'when I felt a
hand on my shoulder. I turned round and saw that it was a
policeman. He was arresting me for wanking [masturbating].'

Nowadays you almost have to be careful about rubbing
sun cream on your partner's bottom lest your actions be con-
strued as a lewd act and duly punished. And the penalties can
be harsh. Although difficult to obtain an official tariff, apparently a public blow job incurs a fine of around 1,500 euro and
a possible appearance in court. To be on the safe side, expect
all other acts in your sexual repertoire to be at least as costly.

But don't think the beach is completely puritanical during the policed periods. Much as in *Les Gendarmes de Saint-Tropez*, people have learned how to take great fun in playing games of cat-and-mouse with the CRS. Couples still sneak into the dunes, single guys still dutifully follow, and the whole lot then play hide'n'seek when the CRS launch a foot or horse patrol. Caresses on the beach, like school kids passing notes under desks in physics class, are mischievously subtle but still common enough.

The single men remain undeterred in their pursuit of gratification. For instance, when on-the-spot fines were introduced for anyone caught with an erection, ingenious woodsmen would hang hats on their manhood. Another method would be to cover one's groin with a towel, a jest which became such a matter of habit that some would automatically reach for the towel *whenever* they got up. The police were sadly mistaken if they thought that they could ever dampen the spirit of horny men.

Approaching couples without being noticed by the police became a full-blown military exercise that involved wriggling on one's belly, sometimes for several metres, to get within suitable viewing range of the target. Once in place, some would dig small holes in the sand for relief rather than play with themselves in full view of the binoculars. Farcical? Perhaps. But for participants and spectators such games can be an entertaining substitute for the open sex, which still takes place on the swingers beach before the police arrive and as soon as they leave.

The police also are a presence around the nudist resort at night. In recent years, they have been joined by private security guards employed by groups of property owners for much the same reason that the mayor of Agde sent in the CRS. These guards patrol the apartment complexes and car parks and are equally conscientious in doing their jobs.

'It was a warm evening and we thought that it would be nice to take some air on the terrace before going to bed,' Ross from Montréal (Canada) remembers. 'Françoise was sitting fully clothed on my lap giving me a hug when a bright light was shone in our faces. "Ça c'est pas permis [that is not allowed]," said the guy holding the torch [flashlight]. His other hand held a rottweiler.'

Opinions differ as to the merits of the increasing security in Cap d'Agde. Some (mainly the die-hard naturists) welcome it, and others (mainly the libertines) think the policing has gone too far and any more will jeopardise the unique personality and wide-ranging appeal of the Cap. Despite what the media might say, Cap d'Agde is no longer the outdoor sexual playground it once was. And the principal reason for this change is the heightened security.

Chapter 3

The Naturist

Perhaps the real naked truth about Cap d'Agde is that, despite its sexy reputation, naturists in the purest sense of the word do still exist there. Not only that, they seem to be winning the war against the libertines, convincing the authorities at least that the Cap's future lies down the straight and narrow path of wholesome family holidays, pétanque competitions, and convivial karaoke evenings at Johnny Wokkers Euro Pub. These reasons might not be why *you* have come to Cap d'Agde, and they certainly don't drive the resort's economy, but for many visitors the charm of Cap d'Agde remains simple and wholesome.

Naturists can also appreciate Cap d'Agde's unique personality and value, as the libertines do, and its general acceptance of all types of people.

'Cap d'Agde was the first time for us, but we are used to visiting nude beaches all over Europe and in our country of course where it is very usual,' say Yvon and Max from Amsterdam (Holland). 'The big positive difference for us is that here you don't have to leave the complex, you can walk all day nude and the beach is nearby—it's a little nude town. We think it's a very special spot in the world. People respect each other. If you want to make contact with other couples, there are plenty of possibilities; but if you don't, it's also okay. There is much love, peace, respect, and happiness. You feel it—it's in the air. John Lennon would have liked it, too, I'm sure. Just enjoy the basic elements (and most important things in life): sun, sea, sex, and love.'

And don't think that the Cap d'Agde atmosphere inspires people only to perform physical acts of love. 'Our most special time during our trip occurred on May 2,' remembers Tracy and Michael from Massachusetts (USA). 'It was Mike's birthday and we celebrated with a nice home-cooked dinner, wine, and a walk on the beach. It was a beautiful setting and a romantic night. After a bit of a walk, we sat on the beach and Mike proposed. It was incredibly romantic.'

Even with all the activities on offer in Cap d'Agde, the greatest temptaion is to simply relax and watch the world go by.

This special aura, combined with a nudist infrastructure second to none, continues to attract naturists of all styles, from hippies to die-hards (known as *bios* in French), making Cap d'Agde the most complete naturist centre in the world today.

Good, clean family fun

Although no one argues that the fame of Cap d'Agde is due to its country club-style facilities, splendid golf courses, magnificent diving opportunities, wonderful children's entertainment, and non-stop fun, activities around the resort do involve more than just sex. But the Cap is not a naked Disney World, so don't expect to be spoiled with choice when looking for things to occupy you and the kids. On the other hand, the fact that nothing is forced down your throat—unlike at many other resorts—is a positive for many visitors.

Getting wet—in the biblical sense

The **beach** is—and always will be—the main reason why naturists return year after year to Cap d'Agde. Despite the attention given to the swingers beach, most of the seaside teems with naked bodies doing nothing more risqué than playing bat-and-ball, flying kites, and building sandcastles. The family beach stretches from the jetty all the way to the end of the campsite, and during high season it is as busy as any clothed beach anywhere in the world.

At two points along the waterfront—opposite the restaurant L'Horizon (Plage La Méridienne) and the Espace Villa Romaine (Le Galion Beach Club)—comfortable **deck chairs and parasols** in enclosed areas with their own snack bars are available for rent. The rows nearest the sea are the most expensive, though none are really cheap. The advantages are that you don't have to lie on the sand and lug a beach chair back and forth from your lodging each day. Expect to pay around 13 euro per person per day or 22 euro for a couple. You also can rent paddleboats for 16 euro an hour at these 'private beaches'.

Elsewhere, the only beach commerce is in the form of ice cream- pastry-, and doughnut-sellers plying their trade by walking up and down the beach. The musical tones of a woman's voice calling out 'abricot, chocolat' compel many to buy her apricot or chocolate pastries. Most people, though, head to the nearby restaurants or the fridge in their apartments should they feel hungry or thirsty. **Public toilets** (open 11.30–18.30) and cold **showers** (open at all times) are just off the beach next to L'Horizon.

The several **swimming pools** dotted around the resort are the alternative to the beach. Public pools can be found at the following places: Port Nature 1 (L'Akthios), Port Nature 5 (Waïkiki Beach), Port Ambonne, and the Espace Villa Romaine. Private pools, meanwhile, are available for use by guests of Hotel Eve and residents of Port Vénus.

Check the terms and conditions of your apartment rental contract before spending the 8 euro or so to use one of the resort's swimming pools, since free access to the pool closest to your accommodation is sometimes part of the rent. Nudity, of course, is as welcome poolside as it is on the beach. In fact, you stand a better chance of being requested to remove your Speedos at a swimming pool where there is less of a crowd into which to merge than there is on the beach.

The fascination of big metal balls

Away from the fun and games to be had on the family beach, the highlight of which is perhaps the **volleyball** area opposite the Espace Villa Romaine, the activities on offer in Cap d'Agde are hardly cutting edge. This lack could be explained by the fact that nudity and dangly bits do not lend themselves well to most sporty pastimes. Those in the morning **aerobics** classes at the campsite usually choose to cover up the cracks and batten down the excess flesh. Likewise, joggers on the beach are forgiven for wearing shorts or a top, as are the players on the **tennis courts** at the Espace Villa Romaine. On the other hand, the daily **aquagym** (water aerobics) sessions at 11.15 at the Waïkiki Beach swimming pool are tailor-made for nudity. Many would argue that mini-golf is neither appropriate clothed nor naked. Nevertheless, the Espace Villa Romaine has an undulating **mini-golf** course that snakes around the swimming pool should you be desperate for something to do.

Information on what's going on during your stay is available at the hut opposite the Espace Villa Romaine. Some of the activities—such as scuba diving and wall climbing—may take place outside the resort and will not be naturist. This caveat also goes for the windsurfing, jet-skiing, and other water-based activities. If you start from the nudist beach, be sure to confine yourself to the stretch of coast where nudity is allowed.

Of all the Cap's good, clean family divertissements, however, none gets the blood racing like the game of **pétanque.** If you thought that the goings-on at the swingers beach were heated, you have yet to witness a pétanque competition held on the gravel squares next to the 1664 Café in Héliopolis or between the campsite and the beach. This apparently sedate game played by apparently sedate people has a habit, rather like Monopoly, of becoming fiercely competitive. This passion will bemuse the casual observer, for whom the idea of throwing a big metal ball at a little wooden ball will seem rather like a game of marbles. Heathens! Pétanque is played with *boules* (the famous metal balls) and a *cochonnet* (like a jack in bowling), normally between teams of two or three people throwing a total of almost always 12 *boules*. The idea of the game is to toss your *boules* as close to the *cochonnet* as possible by throwing them from a distance of 6m to 10m. One point is scored for every *boule* you manage to throw closer to the *cochonnet* than your adversary, and the winner is the first to reach 13 points.

Finding a game in the resort isn't difficult. The best places to go, even when no organised competitions are going on, are the 1664 Café in the late afternoon and the section of the campsite between the last row of sites and the beach.

For the kids

Nothing stops the kids trying their hands at pétanque, enjoying some beach volleyball, and even a few holes of mini-golf. Teenagers expecting a range of activities aimed specifically at them, though, will be disappointed. Some half-hearted attempts at kiddies' entertainment exist, notably in the form of a carousel, a bouncy castle, and video games at Héliopolis, and the low-key distractions offered at the campsite.

Youngsters, however, will have most of their fun on the beach. At night during high season the campsite organises open-air discos, complete with dry ice and foam, which gives adolescents the chance to have a few glasses of pop and develop holiday romances. These few tame diversions are yet another indication that Cap d'Agde is not really focused on kids.

In the absence of a formal crèche in the resort, your best bet for finding a **babysitter** is to check the notice boards at the supermarkets and commercial centres for people offering their services.

Good, clean adult fun

Away from the great melting pot of the beach, when the lights go down and the clothes go on, you start to see why people have come to Cap d'Agde. And just as a *bio* who insists on remaining naked 24 hours a day stands out like a sore thumb in a bar such as the Melrose, there also are places where the thong-clad masses of thrill-seekers are outnumbered—or at least equalled—by the naturists. Naked people are the exception rather than the rule at night. This was a slight disappointment for the visitor who posted the following report on www.netnude.com: 'The only major negative about Cap d'Agde is that everybody wears clothes starting at dinnertime (around 8 p.m.). The French like to dress up for dinner. I have no problem with people wearing clothes at night (there were a few nights when it was *way* too cold to go nude). It's just that you will feel out of place being nude at night at the restaurants and clubs.'

The **1664 Café** (04 67 26 34 93) in Héliopolis is one of the best examples of a naturist-friendly place to knock back a pastis or two after a hard day on the beach. The outside terrace at the northern end of the shopping centre is an excellent place for people-watching, and if you get bored of that, you can always turn your eyes towards one of the genteel pétanque games, which are invariably in full swing around this time in the adjacent gravel square. The atmosphere is no less wholesome at night, when an electric keyboard is set up in the café and local entertainers play Edith Piaf and Charles Aznavour covers to a hand-clapping, toe-tapping crowd of grinning 70-somethings.

Along with the 1664 Café, there are one or two other good places to enjoy a sundowner. The high stools on the elevated terrace at **Waïkiki Beach** (04 67 26 32 34) in Port Nature 5 provide an excellent vantage point from which to sip cocktails and, in the absence of a clear view of the sunset, watch the equally impressive transformation of Cap d'Agde-by-day to Cap d'Agde-by-night. **Bar du Port** has a terrace overlooking Port Ambonne, although its position at the intersection of two busy roads makes it a noisier choice than the 1664 Café or Waïkiki Beach.

On the face of it, **Johnny Wokkers Euro Pub** in Port Nature 1 is your archetypal tacky tourist watering hole. Dig a little deeper, however, and you find that the pub is, in fact, your archetypal tacky tourist watering hole with karaoke evenings thrown in for good measure. If you want a reminder of what the Cap nightlife once was, come here. You'll find a bastion of good old-fashioned naturist values, reassuring pints of Guinness, and pot-bellied naked people drinking them. Johnny Wokkers is so popular with naturists and libertines alike because it is the most anglophone place in the whole resort. The pub is British-owned, and as a result has become the meeting place for English-speakers and those in need of a quick fix of Anglo-Saxon culture. Brits, Americans, Dutch, and Germans clearly outnumber the French here.

Despite the live music on offer at the 1664 Café, and in the unlikely event that the karaoke at Johnny Wokkers gives you the urge, there is not enough space at either of these two venues to dance. The campsite, on the other hand, does have plenty of space, but the ballroom dancing evenings held a couple of times a week may be of limited appeal if you are a day under 120.

For a proper boogie, you'll have to go to the two dance venues in Port Ambonne. **La Palmeraie** (04 67 26 28 93) arguably attracts a slightly older clientele, perhaps by virtue of the live music provided by the crooners you saw at the 1664 Café the night before. Next door, **Le Yanka** (04 67 26

79 16) is more of a traditional disco, pumping out the latest tunes until 04.00 or 05.00 at weekends. Popular with locals, resort workers, gays, and single guys who can't get into the swinger clubs, plenty of cruising goes on, even if nothing overtly sexual takes place.

If La Palmeraie and Le Yanka are the naturist's alternatives to the swingers clubs, then the **Sauna Finlandaise** (04 67 01 47 26) in Port Soleil is the cleaner version of the resort's two sexy saunas (see page 123). Naturists have been given the short end of the wedge.

In comparison with the other saunas, the Sauna Finlandaise is tiny and a lot less luxurious, consisting of a makeshift four-person sauna, a TV room, a couple of showers, and a toilet in what feels like someone's house. This ambiance makes it an expensive place to go just to build up a sweat and watch the afternoon soap operas. On the plus side, the sauna—perhaps on account of its size—is nice and warm. The Sauna Finlandaise is open daily from 11.00 to 19.00; on Fridays from 20.00 to 24.00 it is reserved exclusively for women. Entrance costs 15 euro for singles and couples.

Chapter 4

The Libertine

'Libertine' is not a word you hear too often—particularly not when describing the type of people who lead non-conformist sexual lifestyles. 'Wife-swapper', 'swinger', 'lifestyler', and more recently 'playcouple' is the current lingua franca, and 'libertine' seems only to make the odd guest appearance in the racier Victorian novels and serious sociology textbooks. But for our purposes, this literal translation of the French noun *'libertin'* (someone who gives free rein to lust) is the best way to describe the thousands of people who descend on the Cap every year primarily for sex.

'Libertine' works so well because it has different meanings to different people. A libertine is someone who enjoys swapping wives. She also is the wife who enjoys swapping husbands. The husband and wife who enjoy watching husbands swap their wives. The swapped wife who is watched. Husbands who swap husbands. Wives who swap wives. A libertine is a swinger, a lifestyler, a playcouple, an exhibitionist, a voyeur, a fetishist, a frustrated porn queen, a dirty old man in a raincoat, a gang-banger, a polygamous faggot, a slut, a floozy, a nymphomaniac. And Cap d'Agde is where the libertines of the world must come at least once in a lifetime. Nowhere on Earth will you feel so at home expressing your perversions and acting out your fantasies. And so what if the heightened security in recent years (see *Les Gendarmes du Cap* on page 67) has made the Cap somewhat less wild? This place is still unique.

This chapter addresses swingers: couples looking for

ways to spice up their traditional, monogamous sex lives, which often involve finding new partners to play with. Activities for the other libertines—singles and gays—are described in Chapters 5 and 6.

It's a beach, Jim, but not as we know it

Who knows whether the first people who stumbled across this isolated stretch of beach in the 1950s and decided to sunbathe on it naked were swingers. What we do know is that this same stretch of beach, starting where the campsite ends and extending about 300m in front of some sand dunes, has become the meeting place par excellence for the libertines who visit the Cap, a large number of whom are swinging couples. Thus, this area is called the 'swingers beach'. And just as the whole of Cap d'Agde started from here all those years back, the sexy reputation of the place has been built on many a sweaty afternoon romping around these few square metres of sand.

You will hear and read a lot of crap about what goes on here. The main confusion lies in distinguishing between what *used* to happen and what happens today. Libertines were initially attracted to this locale on account of the cover provided by the trees, bushes, and dunes behind the beach itself. Known in gay circles as *Le Petit Bois Joli* (The Pretty Little Wood), this area was a hive of naughty activity in the mid-1980s. Couples, gays, and singles would play more or less undisturbed by the prying eyes of other naturists and the law.

'Someone even built a villa in the dunes without authorisation from the local authorities,' remembers J from Béziers (France), who has been coming to Cap d'Agde for more than 20 years. 'Couples would climb up a ladder to the terrace, push the ladder away, and start having sex. In no time at all, men would be climbing up drainpipes, trees—anything—to get a look.' [He giggles.] 'At around this time a Dutch guy had sculpted a huge phallic symbol on one of the trees, and women literally lined up to have their pictures taken sitting on it. Then a pissed-off naturist cut it off—the penis on the tree, I mean—and the villa got pulled down.'

Worse, however, was to come. Not content to keep the games in The Pretty Little Wood, a new breed of pseudo-libertines eager for titillation at any cost started to express their sexuality on the beach itself in full view of naturist families and their children. Complaints naturally followed, and around the mid-1990s the police arrived on the swingers beach to keep it clean during the busiest time of the year (July and August).

Compared with the orgiastic behaviour of the pre-police days, the swingers beach today is calm. During July, August, and early September, you will probably see nothing out of the ordinary. Couples will have read the hype and rushed to the Cap to see if it is true, not realising—or not being told in the article they have read or the TV show they have seen—that police binoculars and horses have put an end to all but the most innocent of contact. In fact, given the often over-zealous enforcement of the hands-off rules by the police, during high season the swingers beach has in many respects become more puritanical than a Sunday School outing (see *Les Gendarmes du Cap* on page 67).

What you can expect during this period is a lot of eye contact and innocent flirting (which can be a lot more exciting than having a couple masturbate to gain your attention). For even if the police loom large in the background, the swingers beach is still the place where libertines come to meet fellow libertines. Indeed, in some ways the police presence increases the sexual tension.

Everyone knows why they have come to this particular stretch of beach, and the eyes made at other couples are as if to say: 'If these hairy policemen weren't here, we'd jump on you guys.' The sexual current on the swingers beach during the height of summer is understated—but crackling nonetheless. You can woo other couples using good old-fash-

ioned techniques of seduction: eye contact, charm, and suggestive conversation.

And the choice of people will live up to your and, as impor-
tantly, your partner's expectations. For this high season time
of year attracts the younger, better looking crowd. Not always
the most friendly and approachable people in the world, but
nevertheless they are there, like you, to party. And the swingers beach is the best place to make initial contact and lay the
seeds that could later bear fruit in the form of a private party
invitation or a sweaty rendezvous in one of the clubs.

Sex on the beach is not just a cocktail

'What's going on over there, dear?'

'What's that, dear?'

'Over there! What's that crowd of people doing? Do you
think there's been an accident?'

'No, dear, they're just buying ice creams. Now let me go
back to sleep.'

These must be some damn good ice creams to encourage
what can sometimes be more than 100 people to make their
purchases all at the same time. And when this crowd breaks
into a round of applause after several minutes of waiting,
you can only assume that the news is good and there are
enough in stock for everyone. Not such as ludicrous scenario, perhaps, if we were in any other place than the swingers beach in Cap d'Agde during the months when the police
are chasing murderers, rapists, and robbers rather than
naughty nudists. Come to Cap d'Agde in March, April, May,
June, late September, and October if you want to see what
all the fuss is about. Come during these months for sex on
the beach.

The crowd of ice cream buyers is watching people doing
explicitly sexual things to one another. These impromptu
sex shows typically start at around 17.00 when the hottest
part of the day has passed and the tension of seeing so many
naked bodies in increasingly suggestive poses has reached
boiling point. Not much is needed to attract a small audi-

ence, the core of which is invariably the posse of single men who can be found on the swingers beach day-in, day-out with dicks in hand on the prowl for some action. These gatherings are actually quite organised, as a curious Chris from Chicago (USA) found out. 'When a performance started, hoards of men would gather, sometimes three- and four-deep, in a respectable circle to watch. Nosey women such as myself were allowed a front-row view: the French men would say "Veuillez-vous voir? (Do you want to see?)" and make a path for the women.'

An innocent massage, a playful wrestle, a lingering embrace will show up on voyeurs' radar screens and send blood rushing to their nether regions. Some people are amazed to see how long an erection can be maintained simply by watching a couple flicking sand at one another, but such is the power of imagination, optimism, and complete desperation of some people here.

Katherina and Jürgen from Essen (Germany), a couple who enjoy the swingers beach for its open-mindedness rather than from any desire to watch or be watched, remember a spooky guy who took rather a fancy to Katherina. 'We were both reading,' says Katherina, 'when I noticed a man was sitting opposite us. There was much space on the beach but his towel was almost touching ours. It looked like he was staring at me. I couldn't be sure because he was wearing big sunglasses, but he was looking in my direction. Then he smiled and started to touch himself. I looked around to see what he was so excited about, but there was nothing sexy going on. I went back to reading my book and expected this man to lose interest and go somewhere else. But he just kept smiling and playing with himself. This lasted for about 10 minutes before he came. In that time I'd done nothing sexy at all—just turned about four pages of my book.'

Such experiences are not for the easily shockable; and not all will react as phlegmatically as Katherina and Jürgen to such a flagrant breach of their personal space. On the other hand, some couples positively welcome an audience. Discerning whether those participating in sex on the beach are doing it for the attention or because they have an irresistible urge to touch and be touched by whoever they are with is difficult (probably a bit of both come into play). What is certain, however, is that on a good day you will see enough shows to make a reasonable porn film. The following is a list of the type of acts you stand to witness, in descending order of frequency:

- **Couples masturbating**—either themselves or each other
- **The licking of breasts and sucking of nipples**—either by a man or another woman
- **Cunnilingus**—again, performed by either a man or another woman
- **Blow jobs**—almost always performed by a woman (head to the dunes for the gay stuff—see page 161)
- **Sixty-nine**—also known as the *soixante-neuf*; once again, either with a man and a woman or two women
- **Intercourse**—happens less on the beach now than it did a few years ago, but still relatively common in the sea and the dunes
- **Gang-bangs**—prevalent if you include the multiple sucking of penises in the job description
- **Cum shots**—if ever a sexual act was made for public consumption, this is the one
- **Anal sex**—rare, but not unheard of
- **Golden showers**—in the dunes, and usually administered by beefy, pierced Germans
- **The miscellaneous**—and bizarre: 'When I saw a man's entire hand disappear into his lady's private parts, and then he slapped his other hand on his thigh to remove the sand and dived in two-handed, I must admit I cringed,' says Chris from Chicago (USA).

Along with the beach itself, the dunes continue to be a popular venue for sex shows. Less obvious, but also busy, is the sea. About 25m out is a sand bar that allows you to stand ankle-deep in water. This shallow point provides a natural stage for exhibitionists, and crowds can sometimes be seen gathering offshore.

'Do you think there's been an accident, dear?'

'No, they're just fishing. Now let me go back to sleep.'

The end of June and the second half of September are the kinkiest times, due to the sizeable crowd and good weather. The nicer days earlier and later in the season also will be worth a few decent shows, especially on weekends when many local couples come to the beach. Couples may also wish to adapt their wooing techniques to take the sexual freedom at these times into account. Genital contact and eye contact go together in certain situations, so don't be afraid to touch your parts as a way of showing your interest in a couple who are doing the same thing whilst giving you suggestive looks a few parasols away.

But the swingers beach has no secret codes regarding sexual preferences, contrary to the myth revived in a 2002 report in a leading French magazine for swingers. If, as was suggested in the report, a woman lying on her back with legs slightly spread is eager for cunnilingus or vaginal penetration, and a woman on her front with legs slightly spread is after anal sex, then a woman who simply wants to sunbathe with a good book should perhaps adopt the lotus position—or safer still, just stand up. Cap d'Agde is unconventional, but such ideas are going a little too far into the realms of fantasy.

Couples who stroll in the dunes will be followed by a procession of single men as a matter of course. Ignore them if you are simply there, like them, to check out what's going on. If, on the other hand, you are looking to play, the further into The Pretty Little Wood you go, the more privacy you will have. Some have laid the blame for the crackdown in Cap d'Agde squarely on the shoulders of the single men, and some men *have* acted—and continue to act—with startling disrespect (see Chapter 5 on page 137).

Nevertheless, couples seldom report any physical aggression and a polite but firm 'no' works as well on the swingers beach as it does in the swingers clubs and elsewhere in the resort. Even so, exercise caution and common sense in secluded areas such as The Pretty Little Wood.

Grooming for success

Many are fatalistic about looking sexy in a nudist resort, adopting the attitude that you are what you are when you have no clothes on and anything short of plastic surgery is not going to change that. To a certain extent, this mass resignation to the physical imperfectness of all human beings is the great attraction of naturism. Few people look at your rolls of fat or flat chest with a judgmental eye, because they themselves are insecure about some part of their body. This general acceptance is as prevalent in Cap d'Agde as it is at non-sexual naturist centres, and you will feel absolutely no pressure to conform to a certain look.

The Cap's libertine population, though, does not always live by such a philosophy. Whether they are naked on the beach or wearing clothes at night, the aim is always to look as sexually appealing as possible given the raw materials they have to work with.

Smooth, well-oiled machines work best

Back when the libertines first started to arrive in Cap d'Agde, they could always be identified by the lack of pubic hair around their private parts. Nowadays, shaving or otherwise dispensing of such hair has become more widespread, although the libertines continue to lead the way. Other than those behind the dunes in the Réserve Naturelle du Bagnas, you will see few bushes on the swingers beach. The current trend is to do away with the short and curlies altogether, though some prefer to retain a line, a petal, a rectangle, or a V-shaped pair of horns to avoid looking too adolescent.

The other great fashion accessories these days are tattoos and body piercings, both of which are most effective when not hidden under a mound of hair. Tribal designs on the lower back, heel, and groin (for women) and the upper-arm and pecs (for men) were all the rage in 2002, and piercings in a licentious nudist resort tend to end up further south than the bellybutton.

Officially, intimate body piercings and jewellery are not allowed in Cap d'Agde. The campsite has made a special effort to eradicate them. However this rule seems to be universally ignored, and pierced buttons, Prince Alberts, and cock rings are common sightings around the resort.

Many beauty salons offering **hair removal services** for women and men, as well as massages, facials, and other treatments have sprung up around the resort. Shop around for the best deals. At the **tattoo and body piercing** studios, you should also make enquiries as to the hygiene of the establishment. The massages on offer at the salons are for relaxation purposes only. Other masseurs—especially in Port Soleil—offer both therapeutic and more erotic services. Maria and Luca from Venice (Italy) recommend **Paul Massage** (04 67 01 53 02) in Port Soleil by giving a languorous sigh and a broad grin rather than a detailed description of what he actually does.

Free massages, meanwhile, are administered by single men on the beach as a way of ingratiating themselves with couples. Although the quality is variable, this method also is a good way to vet potential partners after feeling how they connect with your flesh. Some women won't even consider sleeping with a man until they have seen him move on the dance floor; in Cap d'Agde, ask for a massage.

Kinky is cool

When you are naked all day, a bit of imagination is sometimes needed to trump that and transform yourself into an even more desirable object when going out at night. Some don't need to try hard. One Cap d'Agde regular has roses tattooed all over her body, which, in dim light, looks as though she is wearing a see-through dress. Middle-aged men with baby fetishes need only slip on a nappy and they are all set; and the heavily pierced may prefer to don some eye-catching chains and baubles instead of hiding their jewellery under fancy outfits.

For others, though, half the fun of coming to Cap d'Agde is the nightlife; and half the fun of the nightlife is dressing up in clothes that you never thought would be seen beyond your bedroom door. 'When I first came to the Cap, I thought it would be quite hard to go naked on the beach,' says Sarah from Essex (U.K.).' It was my first time in a nudist resort, and I was very shy about letting other people see what I looked like in the flesh. And when my husband said that I should pack my fishnet catsuit—something I'd only ever worn in front of him—I nearly died. Talk about running before you can walk! But when I arrived and saw that everyone was sunbathing naked, it seemed silly not to join them. And after a couple of nights out, I soon abandoned the sensible clothes and got out the catsuit. It would've been rude not to!'

You'll see no limit to the styles of dress on show around the nudist resort at night. If nudity is permitted everywhere and at all times, no one is going to reprimand you for wearing an outfit that is too revealing—except, perhaps, the Mistral wind. The following represents the tip of the iceberg for styles of dress on display after dark in Cap d'Agde:

- **Classically sexy**—Little black dresses; evening gowns with high-rising slits; half-buttoned silk shirts; lace lingerie; designer boxers
- **Classically slutty**—Mini-skirts; hot pants; mesh muscle shirts; stockings and suspenders (garters); thigh-high platform boots; glow-in-the-dark g-strings; leopard-skin briefs
- **The fetishist**—Anything in leather, PVC, vinyl, rubber, and the like; military uniforms; police uniforms; doctors and nurses; teachers and schoolgirls; jodhpurs and whips and saddles and stirrups for trainer and pony-boy/girl; nappies (diapers) and a strong safety pin

- **The cross-dresser**—For men: Any of the classically sexy or slutty female attire mentioned previously; one of Auntie Matilda's frumpy dresses with a floral design; For women: Tuxedo with a bow tie but no shirt

Of all the boutiques in Cap d'Agde, those selling kinky outfits, sexy lingerie, and raunchy footwear are the most popular. Shopping for slutwear has become an integral part of the Cap's nightlife. And the erotic fashion shows in the restaurants, bars, and clubs are intended by the organisers primarily as a means of publicity as opposed to titillation. Indeed the trade in lingerie, leather, PVC, vinyl, latex, spandex, and the like is brisk, and the choice can seem overwhelming.

The best place to go for a general idea of what's on offer is Testosterone Corridor, where every other shop seems to be selling raunchy clothing. At the entrance to the corridor on the Port Ambonne side, **Boutique Fantasy** (04 67 21 40 90) has as good a selection as anywhere else. Both this store and **Fantasy II** next to the entrance to Le Glamour are the Cap d'Agde branches of the well-known Parisian boutique of the same name, which is perhaps why prices tend to be on the expensive side. Most of what is sold at Boutique Fantasy, including an impressive array of high-heeled shoes and boots, is for women. A little further down the corridor, however, at **Séduction Styl'** (04 67 26 91 60), you can find plenty of stuff for men. At the other end of the corridor, the friendly **Tara Studio** (04 67 94 14 31), though considerably more conservative than most boutiques in the resort, does have a good range of reasonably priced shoes and jewellery.

More or less next door in Port Nature 5, **Vero Over** (04 67 77 23 64) specialises in fetish clothing, with various leather, rubber, and other such outfits for him and her created by designer, Véronique (there is another Vero Over in Port Nature 1). Although the quality of some clothes and accessories on sale in Cap d'Agde is often only average, the lingerie sold at **Hélé** (04 67 21 10 82) in Héliopolis is by top-notch names such as La Perla from Italy, Neyret from France, and Hanro from Switzerland, and is the place to go if you have a bit of cash to spend on something that you would like to still be in one piece when you return to the Cap next year.

In addition to the places mentioned above, other boutiques, principally in Port Nature and Port Ambonne, offer that spiked bra you've always been looking for or a pair of crotchless panties for Auntie Matilda back home. Shop around for the best deals—and have no delusions as to the quality of the item you are purchasing.

Boutiques in the resort are typically open from May to September at some point during the day and from 17.00 to 02.00. 'Many of these shops don't open til late afternoon or early evening and they do a brisk business,' says one Cap d'Agde trip report posted on the Internet. 'The person with the leather studded collar, complete with leash, being led by a "friend" was evidence of that.'

Your place or mine?

Having used your immaculate grooming and irresistible personalities to lure a nice couple (or couples) on the beach, you basically have two ways of socialising of an evening in Cap d'Agde: either you can hit the bars and clubs (see page 95) or you can meet up with your new-found friends at private gatherings. Although the higher quality encounters take place behind closed doors, not to visit a swingers club at least once during your stay would be a pity. Guests at a private party have usually been chosen because they are all likely to get on, both in a social and a sexual sense. And those in attendance probably want to play, which is not always the case at sex clubs. And although a few swingers prefer to know nothing about the people with whom they are swinging other than what turns them on sexually, the majority likes to build a rapport before jumping into bed.

A few drinks on the terrace and maybe even a plate of pasta together provides a great opportunity to continue where you left off on the beach, get comfortable with people you don't know all that well, flirt a little, and then take the party from there. Sometimes this next step means going as a group to a swingers club to finish off the evening; other times you'll want to stay at home for a spot of dessert.

Staying at home has advantages over a club. You avoid sweaty, crowded, and slippery playrooms for the luxury of clean sheets and proper mattresses. You have your sex toys close at hand, may bring a camera or a video recorder, and can play in the knowledge that you will at least know the identity of the person fondling your tits.

Taking a peek behind closed doors

Private parties (a rather misleading term, since rarely do they involve much dancing, drinking to excess, or other traditional party behaviour) typically kick off at around 19.00 or 20.00, giving guests enough time to get home from the beach, shower, shave, and dress.

An *apéro* is a pre-dinner cocktail and can be an ambiguous word in Cap d'Agde. Sometimes an invitation to 'boire l'apéro avec nous (have a pre-dinner cocktail with us)' is nothing more than that. The couple may want to know you a little better before inviting you for a full-blown session, or maybe nothing more daring than a conversation about whether pétanque should be played in teams of two or three will have crossed their minds. This potential confusion makes planning your dress for such an evening a delicate affair.

Best, perhaps, to err on the side of caution, going for the little black dress and thong rather than the see-through bodice sans panties. You will have a clearer idea of where the evening is going if you are hosting the *apéro*, although again you should bear in mind that your guests might not necessarily be on the same wavelength as you.

Couples can also use the *apéro* as a byword, much like the 'do you want to come back to my place for a coffee' line used in conventional dating scenarios, to invite a couple or a single guy to come directly from the beach to their apartment. This type of cocktail is usually a prelude to sex, as it was for Mandy and John from Ontario (Canada), who took a fancy to a swarthy Italian guy on the swingers beach. 'We were slightly embarrassed to ask him back to our place for sex, so we invited him for a drink. When we got to the apartment, we realised we hadn't even got a bottle of water in the fridge. We had a little laugh about it, and then we dragged him into the bedroom.'

A dinner invitation also can mean different things to different people. However, here the chances are that your swingers beach buddies—who have found you to be attractive enough to invite for a dinner which, in France at least, could go on for a few hours—will be hoping for an erotic end to the evening. Come armed with plenty of pétanque small talk nonetheless. And always be polite and bring a bottle of wine or some other offering such as a dessert. Assuming the dinner party will not just be an orgy of fine French cooking, the following gives you some idea of what to expect:

19.38: You knock on the door of apartment 407 in Port Nature. Husband is wearing his favourite white satin trousers and a tight-fitting crimson muscle shirt, and you have chosen a classy black robe: ankle-length on one side, hip-length on the other. Husband presents the host with a fluffy lemon meringue, accompanied by a grin oozing with innuendo.

19.39: You are invited into the apartment. You are the last couple to arrive—predictable seeing that you were told to come at 19.00. You were waiting in the bar opposite the apartment monitoring the other guests as they arrived before you decided to go for it. At first glance, your prudence seems to have been rewarded. The other couples all look okay.

19.45: Drinks in hand, you start to mingle. The hostess has done this before and introduces you to the couple you expressed an interest in meeting on the beach earlier on in the day. They look slightly different with clothes on: husband thinks that the woman looks slimmer; you think that the man looks more sensitive. Either way, the thoughts are encouraging.

20.08: Conversation is still going strong when everyone is told that dinner is ready. The seating arrangements are informal, the only apparent rule being that a man sits next to a woman who sits next to a man and so on. Husband is at the end of the table; you are sitting next to him, with the host next to you on the side where your dress is slit up to the hip.

20.15: Ham and melon is served as a starter. The conversation is somewhat difficult for you to follow—something to do with sheep, and you guess that the main course must be lamb. Husband's French is worse than yours, and he has no idea what they are talking about. He assumes the conversation must have something to do with sex, and his boyish excitement is reflected in another lemon meringue grin. You hope that at least one of the ladies present will find this grin a turn-on—because you certainly don't. You kick him under the table.

20.18: You kick him again before he helps himself to another slice of melon without first having been offered one.

20.49: The main course turns out to be duck.

21.02: You listen patiently as the host explains in broken English how he and his wife got into the lifestyle. 'We av soirées like zis often but I never see woman beautiful as you.' With that you feel his hand on your thigh. Of course, he's full of shit, but you're not altogether turned off by his advances. It must be the accent.

22.07: You mime the words of 'Happy Birthday to You' in French. The table is cleared for what must be the cake, but instead a naked woman (one of the guests) enters from the bathroom and clambers onto the table. The hostess sprays the guest's nipples and groin with whipped cream and sticks three candles into the white foam. The birthday boy blows out the candles and proceeds to lick cream off his wife's left nipple.

22:08: Other guests (male and female) help themselves

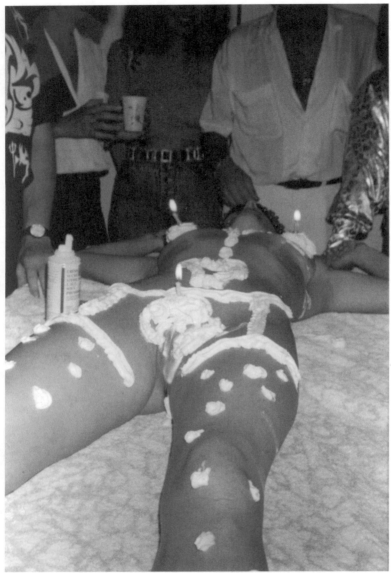

Depending on how well people know one another, private parties in Cap d'Agde can start off awkwardly. But nothing breaks the ice like a can of whipped cream, three candles, and a little imagination.

to a slice of the human cake.

22.12: Husband whispers in your ear that this would perhaps be a good time to suggest a game of naked Twister.

On your other side the host now has his hands inside your panties, so you tell husband that you think it's too late for that as you wipe whipped cream off your earlobe.

22.20: The hostess spills wine on husband's white satin trousers as she tries to open his fly with her teeth. He hides his irritation surprisingly well, even though he'll be nagging you about it for the rest of the holiday.

23.32: The six of you agree on a timeout for a glass of champagne. The hostess goes to procure the glasses, the couple with whom you were talking before dinner starts to dress (their babysitter is due to leave at midnight), and husband and the host rub your shoulders. *La vie est belle!*

23.34: The champagne arrives in the nick of time, since you were in danger of dosing off in the arms of these two hunks.

00.00: Instead of turning into a pumpkin, your second wind kicks in and the games recommence.

00.47: As you sip another glass of champagne and smoke a cigarette naked on the terrace with the warm breeze of a balmy Cap d'Agde night massaging your exhausted limbs, you understand why you love this place so much. *La vie est belle!*

01.21: You are the last couple to leave. Husband is elated; you are purring inside with satisfaction. All in all, a delightful evening.

Carnal clubbing

The sexy nightlife in Cap d'Agde is legendary. In the early days when the libertines first started to arrive in force, and before the police and private security firms made their rude entrance, this nightlife would slap you in the face as soon as you stepped foot outside your apartment.

The provocative outfits still exist, but back then the whole town was a playground and a swingers club was more a place to go if it was raining and you didn't want to get your expensive lace lingerie wet. The clubs seem to have seen an increase in their popularity as the outside security in the resort has increased. Nowadays you can count on them being packed during high season, which is a good part of their attraction.

At the same time, many old-timers have noticed a change in atmosphere. 'When I first started coming to the Cap—I suppose it was in the late 1980s—the clubs were as much about the seduction as the sex,' reminisces Nathalie from Clermont-Ferrand (France). 'You would come with your friends, have a good dance, a few drinks, and if there was someone you found interesting, things would progress in a natural way to the playrooms. Now you're expected to get down to the sex before you've even had a drink. At one club [Le Glamour] there are even signposts in the playrooms: "Bi-sexuals" go this way, "Threesomes" that way, and "Couples" over there. It's all too regimented for me. It's not sexy.'

Another complaint, somewhat in contradiction to Nathalie's observations, is that people are doing too much watching and not enough doing at many of the Cap's clubs these days. For the libertine who knows no better, however, a visit to a Cap d'Agde swingers club should not be missed.

Bear in mind one or two things when going clubbing in the Cap, which may vary slightly from elsewhere. A distinction is often made in North America between 'on-premises' and 'off-premises' clubs (places where sexual acts are allowed in the club itself and places where they are not); in Cap d'Agde, all clubs are of the 'on-premises' variety where you can purchase alcoholic and non-alcoholic drinks. As far as the dress code is concerned, you will rarely be refused entry for not looking as dapper as James Bond. Men can usually wear jeans and even sports shoes, although shorts—unless they are of the tight-fitting, crotchless, or see-through variety—will probably be censured. Women, meanwhile, should avoid trousers with all but the most daring styles and cuts. Such apparel is considered too frigid in the wacky world of the alternative lifestyle.

The standard club will have a bar and a dance floor, which operate like any disco. This area is the realm of the exhibitionists and the gropers and is where you should woo

You'll find nothing secret about the approach to the *Quartier Naturiste* of Cap d'Agde. You pay your entrance fee and come on in. This nudist section of the resort town Cap d'Agde on the Mediterranean coast is well known.

The beach in August is stuffed with people of all types. For some, the crowd is a delicious meat market; for others, it's a chance to see old friends made over the years. Bring or buy a parasol (umbrella) because the beach has no trees for shade. Some apartments have a parasol as part of the standard equipment. Most folks lie on towels and straw mats on the sand.

The most sociable place in the resort at around dusk is the vast campsite, when the wine and olives are brought out for the ubiquitous *apéritif*. This event is also a great excuse to meet up with like-minded people for a few fun and games after a sexually charged day on the beach.

RIGHT: The Melrose has been surviving for years on prompting customers to give improvised stripteases on the bar and tables. This simple entertainment is often rather more *The Full Monty* than *Coyote Ugly*—but at least it's free.

Despite what the naughty voice inside is telling you, not all displays of affection in the Cap are sexually motivated. If the French can kiss on alternating cheeks (on the face) when greeting and parting, why can't they give one another a friendly hug from time to time?

Despite having to pay to use the resort's several swimming pools, you'll find they can be a good place to meet the Cap's 'beautiful people'. Moreover the odds of meeting single women is better at the pools than at the beach. PHOTO: Don Marcus

A photo of shopping naked in Cap d'Agde is part of most visitors' albums. Seeing people with only shoes and purses is common.

Pizza is one of several fast-food options available in the resort. McDonald's can justify the risk of opening a restaurant in Cold War Russia, but not here.

Expect to enjoy delicious fresh fruits and vegetables all summer long in Cap d'Agde. Sandrine at Les Jardins d'Hélios in Héliopolis is one of the many employees in the resort town.

The *pâtisseries* and *boulangers* (pastry shops and bakeries) often sell picturesque goods to appeal to the naughty natures of many Cap d'Agde visitors.

Looking over Cap d'Agde's Hélio Village (a group of villas/townhouses) is Mont St. Loup (Holy Wolf Mountain), an extinct volcano and one of the few high points easily seen from a very flat Cap d'Agde. PHOTO: Don Marcus

RIGHT: Héliopolis (pictured here from section K), the circular building at the centre of Cap d'Agde, offers quick beach access, as does the campsite. Many rooms above the first floor offer adequate beach views.

Many of the activities for children take place in the middle of Héliopolis (pictured here), on the beach, and at the campsite. PHOTO: Don Marcus

LEFT: Almost every rental has a small outdoor space to enjoy your morning coffee. The hummingbirds that frequent the garden flowers are so tiny you might mistake them for large bumblebees on first glance. The terraces in Hélio Village (pictured here) are all on the ground level.

Hervé from Le Havre has put down his magazine to enjoy the view for a minute or two, although a wide open door, a naked body on a bed, and an unprivate terrace is like a red rag to a bull for voyeurs.

RIGHT: In Cap d'Agde, apartments come in all shapes and sizes, and the décor and furnishings are the unique and occasionally controversial choice of the owners. Sofia and Hervé from Le Havre have managed to make themselves at home in this typically atypical studio. Some couples, though, prefer to rent an apartment sized for four to six people instead of two so they can have more room.

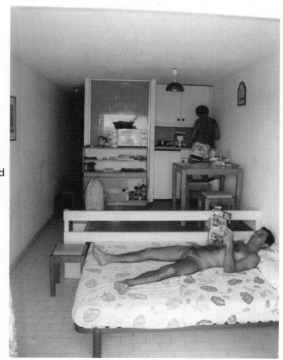

LEFT: Bare buttocks are common in Cap d'Agde, but suggestive peeks remain keenly exciting. Few buildings have lifts, so keep that fact in mind when making your reservations. (The first floor in France is what Americans call the second floor.)

Metal pulldown shutters are typically used to keep interiors cool when residents are out during the day. They also add security against theft. Only a few accommodations have air conditioning, which for the most part isn't needed, especially if your unit has a ceiling fan. Windows don't have screens, so be alert for mosquitos.

RIGHT: Fabie sells shoes and jewellery at the Tara Studio. But visitors could also see her dancing on the bar at the Melrose. Working at the Cap gives people an eclectic CV.

Hélène, the owner of Hélé, one of the more upmarket lingerie boutiques in the nudist resort, greets customers. Americans should remember to be polite by French standards and greet shopkeepers with 'bonjour, madame', or 'bonjour, monsieur', when they enter a small shop. And remember that metallic bikinis are not for the beach.

AIDS awareness is perhaps not as high as it could be in Cap d'Agde. Organisations such as Couples Contre le Sida (Couples Against AIDS) fight the cause with free condoms and gel, and stark reminders that pleasure, too, has its limits.

LEFT: Eric, the owner of Le Look, is friendlier than he looks. His bar, in the heart of Testosterone Corridor, is essentially gay, but as Eric himself is always at pains to point out, he and the bar are open to those of all persuasions.

The sand dunes behind the swingers beach, known in gay circles as *Le Petit Bois Joli* (The Pretty Small Wood), might seem calm enough—indeed, the area is officially protected as a bird sanctuary. But venture into them early or late in the season, and you might hear the chirps and see the peckers of more than just the rare purple heron.

The dunes back the two unofficial naughtier sections of the 2km long nude beach in Cap d'Agde frequented by swingers and gays, unlike the family end of the beach.

Mike and Tracy from Massachusetts got engaged during one trip to Cap d'Agde. They have a website with a section on Cap d'Agde at www.naturistworld.com.

RIGHT: All over Cap d'Agde you'll see posters advertising the bars and sex clubs. PHOTO: Mark Ashworth

Sunbathing is not restricted to the beach. Other idyllic spots, such as this one next to a car park, help visitors escape the crowds.

Bread and a sparkling wine bottle create an alternative to the classic French bra for this silly American gal. The many lingerie shops in Cap d'Agde provide better versions.

The beach's lovely, fine-grained sand can scorch your feet (wear sandals), and sometimes visitors become exhausted brushing it off at the end of the day. Suffer no such problems when you visit one of the many swimming pools. Check your rental agreement to see whether the daily pool fee is already included.

The nudist resort has its own port, Port Ambonne (overlooked in this photo by the Port Nature apartments). Luxurious yachts are also seen from time to time anchored just off shore. Procuring an invite to come aboard is a challenge relished by the 'beautiful people' of the beach.

Most of the beach crowd doesn't go in search of a toilet when all that's needed is a quick pit stop. The clear water is refreshing and usually calm. The sand below the gentle Mediterranean waves is soft on your feet.

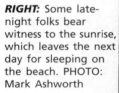

RIGHT: Some late-night folks bear witness to the sunrise, which leaves the next day for sleeping on the beach. PHOTO: Mark Ashworth

your couple—or whoever else interests you. If you get lucky, head for the *coins calins* or playrooms: the nooks and crannies in the more secluded parts of the club, where mattresses and discreet lighting ease inhibitions. Some clubs have other facilities such as glory holes (cubicles with strategically positioned holes in the walls large enough for most body parts), chains, crosses, and other BDSM accoutrements; showers and free condoms are standard at most clubs.

A note for guys who have entered couples-only clubs with a female companion whom they have left running up a bill at the bar while they go and play: clubs in Cap d'Agde are strict about checking that those who enter the playrooms are with someone of the opposite sex.

Dirty dancing

The swingers clubs get going from around midnight onwards. Assuming that dinner is out of the way by about 22.00, you will have a couple of hours to kill before heading to the club of your choice. You could quite easily spend this time hopping from one slutware boutique to another, all of which are open and doing a roaring trade at this hour. The other option is to have a drink at either of the two bars operated by the monopolistic Espace Villa Romaine, which are in reality pseudo-swingers clubs.

Melrose Café

Testosterone Corridor (04 67 81 70 67) Open daily 17.00–02.00; drinks 5 euro (beer), 3,50 euro (soft drinks), spirits & cocktails various prices.

For many, the Melrose Café at the entrance to Testosterone Corridor on the Port Ambonne side will be the first real taste of the Cap d'Agde nightlife. And even if you don't actively search it out, you'll pass it hundreds of times during your stay and be tempted to stop and look on more occasions than you would probably care to admit. For this bar, easily the most popular in the resort, continues to woo customers with a staple diet of naughty entertainment and an ambiance that makes meeting new people easy.

The bar is quite large—covered by a makeshift tarpaulin roof but otherwise open to the elements and dotted with barrel tables in keeping with its underplayed nautical theme—although during August you will not be able to move for the number of people the bar attracts. At this time movement along Testosterone Corridor also grinds to a halt, as people slow to ogle the dancers who use the Melrose's long bar to perform strip routines of various quality.

If one of the boutiques is not holding a fashion show—at which time the male and female dancers will be lithe and sensual—you will be treated to performances by the customers themselves: a motley selection of overweight housewives putting cracks in the barrels with their lumbering moves; frustrated strippers auditioning at the bequest of their proud husbands; eager young guys tempted to join a female dancer in the hope of a few free gropes in the name of art; and, if you're lucky, the magical sight of the incredibly bulky German woman who habitually comes to the Cap in June gliding across the bar with the grace of the prima ballerina hippopotamus in *Fantasia*.

The entertainment is ad hoc and variable, but rest assured that the programme remains the same every night. The drinks, meanwhile, are pricey in comparison with elsewhere—and beware of overcharging.

Photography is officially banned, although the occasional camera is sometimes seen hoisted above heads for a shot of the dancer of the moment—and normally no one seems to mind. Public sex also is forbidden. As a result, when a dancing couple looks as though they might be on the verge of making some oral moves, the DJ quickly restores order with a verbal warning to keep the party clean. Likewise, someone checks the bar itself for overly amorous customers. Touchy-feelie stuff does takes place—it's just more discreet than in the swingers clubs: a hand slipped between an opened fly beneath the table or a stolen lick of a nipple in a dark corner of the bar.

Much to the disappointment of the management and customers alike, local bylaws have meant that the music at the Melrose and other bars along Testosterone Corridor must be turned down at midnight. This rule severely affects the atmosphere and, since this time also is when people are thinking about moving on to the swingers clubs, the bar starts to empty well before the official closing time.

Hemingway Café

Héliopolis (04 67 26 43 39) Open daily breakfast–02.00; drinks 5 euro (beer), 3,50 euro (soft drinks), spirits & cocktails various prices.

Similar to the Melrose in the sense that it attracts the same sort of clientele, the Hemingway Café is a different style of bar: smaller, more intimate, and usually a lot quieter (due in large part to its out-of-the-way location—at least as far as nightlife is concerned—in the Héliopolis shopping centre). This place only seems to rev up during high season; at other times most people go to the Melrose.

The Hemingway Café does have advantages over its sister bar. For a start, being indoors you will not get cold on windy nights (as you can do at the Melrose). Alternatively, air-conditioning will keep you cool when temperatures start to rise. The Hemingway Café has a small dance floor and, since no apartments are above or immediately next to the bar, the music can continue at full blast until closing time. Those people not moving on to the swingers clubs at midnight often end up at the Hemingway Café.

You can buy Cuban cigars here—albeit for 16 euro a time—and the bar is open for breakfast and lunch (continental breakfasts cost 5 euro). A large screen TV lets you watch sports events and, in the evenings, music videos. Minors are allowed in the bar until 21.00.

The Hemingway Café remains faithful to the recipe that has worked so well for the Melrose. It has a long table/small stage in the middle of the bar, upon which sexy fashion show models, exhibitionists, and the bar staff perform their raunchy routines. The music is mainly of the electronic variety, and the clientele often tends to be young and masculine. Indeed, single guys may be refused entry during the busiest times of the year. The same rules regarding public sex apply here as they do at the Melrose—although these rules don't seem to deter the post-adolescent local boys in particular from groping at will. This groping can sometimes make the Hemingway Café feel more like a meat market than elsewhere in the resort.

Choosing a swingers club

Having enjoyed a romantic meal, hopefully featuring oysters, sushi, wine, chocolate, and anything else remotely aphrodisiacal, after which you have spent an hour or two absorbing the high sexual tension that pervades the resort at night, you are now ready to fork out the cash to visit one of the Cap's famous swingers clubs. There were four in the resort to choose from in 2002.

Le Glamour

Espace Villa Romaine (04 67 01 55 49; www.espacevilla romaine.fr) Open every night 20.00–02.00. Couples only (single men allowed Mondays). Admission: 30 euro per couple (46 euro for single men); drinks 8 euro; bottles 77 euro.

All that is good and bad about Cap d'Agde for swingers is encapsulated in Le Glamour, which is the resort's most popular club. First, the good. Along with one or two of the more exclusive clubs in Paris (see page 40), probably nowhere else in the country will you find such beautiful, glamorous people.

One of the main complaints among swingers is the difficulty finding partners who are attractive to *both* sides of the couple. Le Glamour provides the best chance of finding a good match. You'll see no particular style of clientele here, though. The young and beautiful mix with the old and well preserved. Expect something for everyone on any given night.

The interior has also been designed to be as aesthetically pleasing as the patrons who fill it every night, sometimes in the hundreds. The club is large with a good mixture

116

of open spaces (both indoors and out) and intimate play areas. No surprise, then, that Le Glamour attracts thousands of visitors every season.

Popularity, however, breeds contempt, and the more popular the club becomes, the more complacent and arrogant it becomes. The philosophy here is that so long as the beautiful people keep coming and the not-so-beautiful keep forking out their 30 euro admission fee, why bother with customer service? The brute at the door with the social skills of a gorilla (you'll recognise him by his Mike Tyson-esque frown and monosyllabic conversation) will piss off several customers a night, but who cares when people are literally queuing up for entrance? What makes the club's scant regard for its customer's feelings hard to fathom is that quite often Le Glamour fails to deliver the goods. Increasingly, people are coming to watch others have sex rather than do anything themselves, making some nights more like an expensive peep show than a swingers club.

The main part of the club is divided into two bars and a dance floor. The larger of the two bars is outside: a pleasant place to cool off after a turn on the compact, crowed dance floor. Go downstairs for the playrooms: dark, labyrinthine, and deceptively large. A signpost at the bottom of the stairs points you to play areas devoted to couples only, those looking for threesomes, and bisexual swingers. A basket of condoms and a member of staff who checks that the right people go to the right play areas (single men take note) can also be found at the bottom of the stairs.

If you thought the dance floor was busy, the playrooms will seem positively heaving. On closer inspection, however, most of the people will be shuffling along the dark passages like visitors at a zoo, peering at the relatively few people having sex on the beds. Even so, the odour of sweat and love can sometimes be more overpowering than a zoo's elephant house. Considering the number of people who visit the club, the two showers (one each in the ladies' and gents' bathrooms) is woefully inadequate.

Although the normal tariff for a couple is 30 euro, there are cheaper ways of getting into Le Glamour. If both members of the couple take a menu at the Restaurant Villa Romaine (see page 59), club entrance will only cost 9 euro. Alternatively, those who purchase a bottle for 77 euro should be able to enter without paying an admission fee for the next three or four days. Mixers will also be supplied free of charge, and you can bring another couple with you. Note that these rules are liable to change, especially during busy times, and can vary depending on the mood of the staff.

Le Loft VIP

Port Nature 1 (04 67 26 22 10) Open every night from 23.00. Couples only. Admission: 30 euro per couple (65 euro for single men when allowed in); drinks 10 euro (spirits), 8 euro (beer & soft drinks), bottles 95 euro.

With Le Glamour closing at 02.00, the mighty commercial machine that is the Espace Villa Romaine threatens to grind to a halt just when the Cap d'Agde nightlife is in full swing and plenty of money is still to be made. Enter Le Loft VIP, promoted as Le Glamour's after-hours club and owned by, you guessed it, the Espace Villa Romaine.

During off-season, patrons of Le Glamour are given free tickets to continue their evening at Le Loft. In high-season the management hits you for another 30 euro admission charge. As if this liberty weren't enough, a new restaurant called The Living Room opened on Le Loft's premises in 2002 as yet another means of parting you from your hard-earned cash.

Although somewhat smaller than its sister club, Le Loft can become just as congested, especially around 02.00 when people are thrown out of Le Glamour. At this time, the voyeuristic couples, having passed a titillating evening of suggestive dancing in provocative outfits, are usually happy to go home and release their pent-up excitement on one another. The more dedicated swingers finish off the evening at Le Loft. The net result is that Le Loft is often more hard-core than Le Glamour, even if the general age and physical appearance of the people are more in line with the resort's other swingers clubs: middle-aged and not always stunningly good looking.

Immediately after the entrance is a postage-stamp dance floor, behind which are two bars and, right at the back of the club, playrooms where single men are allowed. Upstairs (mind the sloping floor and the step before you reach the stairs) are the playrooms for couples only: basically one large room with about four separate spaces created by partitions. Arrive early rather than later to be sure of finding a (relatively clean) space to play. On the same floor is a lounge with comfy chairs and mellower music for chilling out, as well as the tables and playrooms of the club's new restaurant.

The Living Room is open for dinner from 21.00 to 03.00. If you are dining before Le Loft opens, menus indicate if entrance to the club is included in the price. If you want a meal after the Le Loft has opened, you must first pay the 30 euro to enter the club. The idea is for The Living Room to also open in the afternoons, at which time it becomes a swingers club in its own right. For this purpose, a large tent has been erected in the open air at one end of the restaurant and filled tastefully with beds and mattresses. Three showers have been installed and a transparent water tank—accessible by a ladder, large enough for about four people standing side by side, and illuminated at night—has become the motif of the resort's newest space for swingers. To be fair, they have done a good job with the décor. Note that the facilities of the restaurant become part of Le Loft when the latter opens.

Le Juls

Port Nature 5 (04 67 26 93 26) Open every night from 23.00. Couples only. Admission: 25 euro per couple (with one drink each) or 45 euro (with three drinks each); drinks 8 euro (spirits), 5 euro (beer & soft drinks), bottles 90 euro.

Formerly Le Cléopâtre (the resort's gay and lesbian

swingers club), a newly renovated establishment called Le Juls opened in 2002 on the same premises. (Juls, although not quite as widely known as the beautiful Egyptian queen, is nevertheless a big shot in Cap d'Agde being the owner of another club, Le Pharaon, and a swanky restaurant, Brasserie Le Bistro.) Le Juls occupies the building beneath the

Karen from Montpellier struts her stuff at a fashion show held at the swingers club, Le Juls.

Waïkiki Beach swimming pool and bar in Port Nature 5. This location makes the club appear larger than it is, for the interior, although fresh from renovations, is compact and not large enough to cope with the customers during the busy times.

Le Juls, now a club for heterosexual swingers, is the main competition to Le Glamour. The people who wind up here are, generally speaking, not as beautiful as those who frequent Le Glamour. They are also slightly older. But people come here to swing as opposed to just rock feebly back and forth on a bar stool watching the beautiful girls on the dance floor shake, wiggle, and then go home.

Pound for pound, more actual sex is going on at Le Juls than at Le Glamour. You will also appreciate the more down-to-earth atmosphere that comes with the couple-next-door clientele, as well as the diversity brought by the fair number of lesbians who continue to come here despite the demise of Le Cléopâtre.

The bar is directly opposite the entrance to the club. To your left is the dance floor; to your right the toilets and play-rooms. The space is well designed—for a swingers club, that is. The dance floor is surrounded on three sides by soft chairs for checking out and getting to know the talent and a slightly raised platform with a cage and long mirrors for the show queens (and kings) in the house. The bar is logically positioned between the dance floor and the playrooms, the two places where you are likely to build up a thirst.

The playrooms, however, are where the club risks scoring low marks. They are fine when only a few people are using them: clean enough, a reasonable mix of open spaces and more intimate corners, three good showers with towels and a changing area, and free condoms. Take a look at them at around 01.00 at the beginning of August, though, for a different picture: writhing with bodies, hardly enough space to have sex standing up let alone in the missionary position, and wreaking of bodily fluids. In high season, arrive at Le Juls earlier rather than later and try to be among the first couples in the playrooms. Guys also note that the above information could be a good line of argument to persuade reluctant partners to lose their inhibitions and go to the playrooms without delay in the name of hygiene and comfort if not overwhelming sexual desire.

Le Pharaon

Port Ambonne (04 67 01 39 17) Open every night from 23.00. Couples and single men allowed. Admission: 25 euro for couples (free on gang-bang nights—Tuesdays & Fridays); 50 euro for single men.

Le Pharaon was the first swingers club to open in Cap

Le Pharaon is one of the resort's smaller and older swingers clubs, packed on most nights with single men and couples fond of the 'gang-bang' and other games where testosterone is most definitely king—or should that be Pharaoh? (RIGHT PHOTO: Mark Ashworth)

d'Agde—though back in those days it was called Katy's Club, and the type of swinging that went on was innocent by today's standards. A daring evening at Katy's Club was when a few patrons would turn up wearing thongs; nowadays gang-bangs are more in vogue. For Le Pharaon is the only swingers club in the resort (not counting the Nat Hamman sauna and the gay La Scala—see pages 124 and 163), where single men are accepted. Whatever your views vis-à-vis mixed swingers clubs, the presence of plenty of horny males creates a specific ambiance.

If the incessant pluming of feathers with little follow-through at Le Glamour gets on your nerves, rest assured that people (at least the men) have come to fuck at Le Pharaon. This ambiance, in turn, has attracted a not insignificant number of couples looking for MMF threesomes rather than other couples. Often the club is not bulging with top models, but at least you know what you are going to get. Or do you? Le Pharaon has an ambiguous identity. It seems to switch from being straight to gay from one year to the next; and at the beginning of every season it is certainly gay-friendly.

The interior of the club is dated in comparison with the competition, and the odd Egyptian fresco here and there does little to liven it up. The main room is split into a smallish dance floor and bar (next to the entrance) and an area with chairs and sofas (at the back of the club). The playrooms are basic and functional, but like all of the clubs in the resort much too small to accommodate the heavy traffic during high season.

Blowing off steam

If you don't fancy dressing up to go out, and soaking in a hot tub holds more appeal than knocking back expensive glasses of champagne and letting it all hang out on the dance floor, then you could try one of the resort's two swingers saunas, next door to each other in Port Ambonne. These places see more action in the afternoons than the evenings, particularly when the weather is not ideal for the beach. They are both generally clean and well maintained, although standards inevitably slip when a lot of people are using the facilities. Neither sauna is big enough to cater to the demand during high season.

No dress code exists at either sauna; you undress on entry and spend the rest of the time in a towel, a robe, or naked. Expect background music, a bar serving coffee, soft drinks, beer, and the like, as well as TVs showing adult films. But the main reason to come is for the sauna, steam bath, hot tub, and—depending on who you meet—the playrooms.

Nat Hamman

Port Ambonne (04 67 01 20 31) Open daily 14.00–01.00 in season. Couples and single men allowed. Admission: 31 euro for couples (with one drink each); 35 euro for single men (no drink).

Single guys flock to the Nat Hamman like hogs to water in the hope of finding couples who are looking for MMF threesomes or moresomes. And despite the recent opening of a sauna for couples only, the Nat Hamman's original clientele seems to have remained loyal. As Thierry, the owner of both saunas, explains: 'The type of couple who comes here [the Nat Hamman] is not the type of couple who goes next door [to Le 2 & 2—see page 125]. We still get as many people at the Nat as we have always done.' In other words, you can expect tons of single men and a few couples who have a good idea what they are looking for and are not shy about getting it. Good and bad news, then, for the gentlemen, who will have to fight tooth and nail for their opportunity to be with the active couples. The battle is often won or lost in the large hot tub that can accommodate about 15 people, but often plays host to rather more than that when a couple starts making signs of looking for some male company.

Along with the hot tub is a sauna and a steam bath, both large enough for around 10 people. The playrooms include an open space with a large mattress, a swing and a cross, a small box room with glory holes and a surgeon's table, a room with a window so that the unchosen can see exactly what they are missing, and another with a one-way mirror which, when the lights are turned up, allows everyone in the bar to see what you are up to.

Le 2&2

Port Ambonne (04 67 26 35 52) Open daily 14.00–02.00 in season. Couples only. Admission: 31 euro per couple (with one drink each).

Until the 2002 season, the sauna next to the Nat Hamman was gay. It has now gone the way of most other clubs in the resort and become couples only. A little smaller perhaps than the Nat Hamman, the facilities are essentially the same—except that the hot tub here is only big enough for four people.

The most obvious difference between the two saunas (apart from the clientele, of course) is the décor and the ambiance it generates. Le 2 & 2 seems keen to promote a convivial atmosphere where everyone does everything more or less together. Of the three playrooms, only one has a door with a lock (another does have a door that closes—but it's a cage door). The rest of the club is fitted with plenty of sofas and beds, all in blood-red upholstery. And since the place can fill up quickly (especially on rainy days), couples have little choice but to fool around on these pieces of furniture in full view of anyone who cares to watch. This decor makes Le 2 & 2 something of a cross between a sauna and a conventional swingers club and a good choice for voyeuristic couples.

Sex beyond the resort

If the thousands of libertines in the nudist resort decided to have a night out at its swingers clubs, the queues would be longer than those at Disney World. For this reason, a satellite sex industry has developed in the environs of the resort to cater to the overflow. The sex clubs beyond the resort are not merely places to go if the establishments mentioned above are too busy. In fact, provided that you have a car or be prepared to take a taxi (for none is within walking distance and public transport to them is non-existent), a visit to a club on the exterior is a refreshing change to playing at home. The clientele will not be radically different, but the surroundings and ambiance often is.

L'Extasia

Le Domaine Saint-Jean des Sources, 34850 Pinet (04 67 77 96 46; www.club-extasia.com) Open July & August every night from 23.00; rest of the year Saturday only. Couples only. Admission: 35 euro per couple (with one drink each); drinks 10 euro; bottles 120 euro.

Potentially, at least, L'Extasia is the most remarkable club in Cap d'Agde. It's 12km from the nudist resort, but on a busy night in good weather this club more than any other will remind old-timers why they started swinging in the first place and convince novices that screwing around is the life for them.

Originally a grange, the building and its grounds were converted some 15 years ago into a playground for liberated adults. L'Extasia quickly grew to become one of the largest, busiest, and most raunchy swingers clubs in Europe.

'It was one big orgy,' remembers Richard and ex-rugby player from Perpignan (France). No stranger to getting down and dirty in scrums on the rugby field, Richard no doubt put his experience to good use in the not-too-dissimilar environment of the playrooms at L'Extasia. 'Some nights were like a Bosch painting, but without the blood,' he continues. 'A pile of arms, legs, bums, and boobs. A bit of a free-for-all really.'

These heady days, however, were not to last. The arrival of other clubs in Cap d'Agde and a change of management have reduced the temperature at L'Extasia by several notches. Nowadays the club rarely

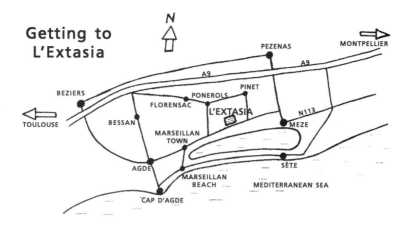

Getting to L'Extasia

seems crowded (a couple of hundred people are not enough to fill the large space here), and theme nights such as those for naturists (Mondays) and fetishists (Wednesdays) have not been enough to incite the wild orgies that were once the club's trademark. Even so, nowhere in the Cap is better suited to large-scale eroticism than L'Extasia.

The particularity of L'Extasia is that as much goes on in the grounds outside as in the club itself. The ground floor of the main building consists of a reception area where you can help yourself to free condoms and enjoy a bar and a compact dance floor. To go upstairs, you have to be in a couple and women must not be wearing trousers. Provided you meet these criteria, you are allowed access to the famous playrooms. The largest is about the size of a basketball court, dotted with flea market-style beds, mattresses, and sofas. Empty it looks like a Salvation Army shelter, and even the presence of several scantily clad women may not be enough to render it more sexy than sleazy. As a result, the more intimate exchanges tend to take place in the cosy spaces created by a maze-like structure of wooden partitions—some with holes for anonymous groping—or up another small flight of stairs in the dimly lit loft. Two showers and plenty of towels are on this floor, which, judging by the odour on busy nights, are underused.

Outside is a long bar next to the entrance to the main building. This bar looks out onto a garden with tables and chairs and an open-air dance floor. At one corner of the dance floor, a gate leads to what for many is the main reason for coming to L'Extasia. *Le Petit Bois* (The Little Wood), not to be confused with the nudist resort's *Le Petit Bois Joli* (The Pretty Little Wood), is a path that leads through the trees where, surprise surprise, people come to fuck. It's best experienced in good moonlight if you hope to see more than the general outline of the person groping your tits. Other than a few low-powered green lights, the wood is not lit.

L'Extasia is a place where actions speak louder than words. Loiter around either of the wood's two sheds filled with the beds not considered smart enough for the main building, and you are sure to feel the wandering hands of another couple before too long. Given the high degree of anonymity under the cover of darkness and the relative ease of getting one's hands on some foreign flesh, The Little Wood is a popular place for couples who may have difficulty finding playmates in the cold half-light of other swingers clubs.

To win back some of the clientele lost to the establishments in the nudist resort, L'Extasia has opened a restaurant, **Le Palaisia d'Occitanie** (04 67 77 16 72), which offers meals combined with tickets for the club, and even a naturist campsite, the **Terre de Soleil** (04 67 77 99 09), which is distinct from L'Extasia in that it follows a naturist rather than a libertine ethic. Only couples and families are allowed at the campsite, and in the absence of a beach it features a large swimming pool as its main attraction.

L'Extasia, Le Palaisia, and the Terre de Soleil are at a place called Le Domaine de Saint-Jean des Sources. The journey takes about 20 minutes by car following the map on page 127.

Le Quai des Anges

Quai du Chapitre, 34300 Agde (04 67 94 88 62) Open July & August every night from 23.00; rest of the year Fri-

days, Saturdays & Sundays only. Couples and single men allowed. Admission: free for couples (with one drink each); 60 euro for single men (with four drinks); drinks 8 euro (spirits), 5 euro (beer & soft drinks).

Along with L'Extasia, Le Quai des Anges is the other main reason to leave the confines of the nudist resort for a sexy night out. Regulars at the swingers beach will have been bombarded with flyers advertising the club's speciality gangbang evenings, although the couples who turn up here are often attracted as much by the free entrance and drinks as the virile charms of 'the gang'. Single guys, therefore, beware of freeloading couples. You can see some action, however, and with so few other places open to single men, it's rather a case of beggars can't be choosers.

This said, Le Quai des Anges does have one of the most attractive interiors of any club in the area. The stone walls and beamed ceilings lend themselves well to the hell-and-purgatory theme, played out fully in playrooms equipped with handcuffs, crosses, and an elaborate pulley system apparently designed for suspending people in mid-air while God-only-knows-what happens to them. The dance floor is of a reasonable size, surrounded by comfortable chairs and, in one corner, a curtain that turns transparent every time the disco lights spin in its direction: a simple yet original aid for voyeurs and exhibitionists. The toilets and two showers, meanwhile, are spotless.

Getting to Le Quai des Anges is a cinch. Make your way to Agde, and instead of crossing the bridge to go to the train station, take the road (Quai du Chapitre) that runs along the banks of the river. The club is 50m or so from the bridge (see the map on page 169).

Le Clan

14 ter Rue de Tunis, 34200 Sète (04 67 53 02 75; www.leclan34.com) Open Wednesday–Sunday 14.00–19.00 & from 21.30. Couples and single men allowed (no singles Saturday evening). Admission: 23 euro Wednesday–Thurs-

day for couples and single men; 30,50 euro Friday–Satur-day (Sundays reserved for private parties).

When you visit Le Clan's website, the welcome page reads simply: 'Etes-vous bi? (Are you bisexual?)'. Only by clicking on 'Oui' will you be taken to the rest of the site. For this club, opened in 2001 in the nearby town of Sète, is one of the few around that caters specially to bisexual swingers, be they female or male. This concept has been earning Le Clan rave reviews. Couples or single men who don't have a bisexual bone in their body will not be turned away, unless they happen to arrive on a night which is officially bisexual (currently Fridays).

Le Clan is what the French would describe as a 'sauna-club'. It has a bar, dance floor, and playrooms like other swingers clubs, but it also has two saunas and a steam bath (with a hot tub coming soon). Anyone interested in visiting Le Clan should call ahead to check on opening times, tariffs, and theme nights, since they tend to change regularly.

For their eyes only: The exhibitionist

How can you be an exhibitionist in a nudist resort? Is anyone going to give a rat's arse if you whip your tits out in a supermarket aisle or flash your pussy in a restaurant? No—but even so, voyeurs are a dime a dozen in Cap d'Agde (*see The World's Biggest Drive-in: The Voyeur* on page 157). So, what are they looking at? To attract attention in the Cap you have to take your nudity, your sexy outfits, your naughty grin, your massive tits, your dick the size of a canoe, your Prince Albert, your studded clitoris, and actually *do* something with them.

Many exhibitionists choose to express themselves on the swingers beach, sometimes quite pornographically. Others prefer to play in the safer environment of a swingers club in the knowledge that many will have come to the club to look at them rather than do anything sexual themselves. Others opt for the thrill of stripping on the bar at the Melrose in front of a cheering crowd. Many possibilities exist for the exhibitionist in Cap d'Agde.

Apartment terraces. The apartment terraces in Port Nature once saw almost as much traffic at night as the swingers beach did during the day. The apartments in Port Nature are particularly well suited to exhibitionism and voyeurism because the terraces can be accessed from public footpaths—in contrast to the balconies at Héliopolis, for example, where spectators only vaguely see what's going on by looking up from the road. The crowds watching the sex on the swingers beach today would huddle round Port Nature's terraces at night, and the resort echoed with rounds of applause at the end of a good show.

Then the more prudish property owners clubbed together to employ private security guards to patrol Port Nature, Hélio Village, Port Soleil, and other residential areas, putting an end to the mass gatherings. Nowadays, although the exhibitionists have not forsaken their terraces, the audience is smaller.

Couples who leave the lights on and the curtains open at night will already be putting out signals, consciously or unconsciously, that voyeurs are welcome. 'It's like in Jaws when Brody was throwing bloody meat into the sea to attract the shark,' says Neil from Chessington (U.K.). The analogy is a good one, for after a while you will notice the fins of several single guys circling your terrace. At this point you have two choices. Non-exhibitionists draw the curtains, annoyed that something so banal could attract so much unwanted attention. But making a big fuss about it will be no more effective than simply showing the sharks that no flesh is here tonight. Next year, of course, you will know to ask for a more private apartment.

On the other hand, exhibitionists will be getting excited by all of the attention. You may want to start proceedings in the apartment itself, just to show the guys that this viewing is not yet another false alarm. The sharks will respond by moving closer to the apartment. You then have the option of moving outside onto the terrace to continue your lovemaking. Someone will likely indicate his desire to join you at some point. Now you are no longer in the realm of exhibitionism and could reply with a firm but polite 'no thanks' if exhibitionism was your sole intent.

Campsite showers. Despite its official policy of reaching out to genuine naturists and clamping down on debauched behaviour, don't think the campsite is a barren land for exhibitionists. Although the high concentration of children ensures that libertines are more reserved than they would be elsewhere, the large shower blocks with doorless cubicles sometimes prove to be irresistible. Indeed for someone who is inclined to exhibitionism, the subtle transition between merely washing yourself and massaging yourself sensually with lathers of shower gel is easy to accomplish, provided a receptive audience is in the cubicle opposite.

Having your partner join you requires more effort, not least because the cubicles are not that large. Since only the person immediately opposite you is able to see what you are doing (a good thing when children are around), showing off in the campsite showers is a bit of a lottery and depends on someone being in the right place at the right time.

The showers are at their busiest from 18.00 to 20.00, when people are coming in from the beach. Kids as well as adults will be washing at this time, so be discreet. From around 21.00 the showers quiet down, and the chances go up that those there are there to play. The shower block on Allée M is the best for exhibitionism. Not only is it the largest, but its rows of cubicles face one another, which is not always the case elsewhere.

Just outside the resort. Exhibitionism takes on a different dimension when you leave the nudist resort. Ironically, people choose to leave a place where they can be naked 24 hours a day to reveal their flesh clandestinely to passers-by. But as practised exhibitionists will tell you, the excitement lies in the knowledge you are doing something naughty and forbidden. For this reason, some of the Cap's exhibitionists prefer to operate just outside the perimeters of the nudist resort, and they are joined by local exhibitionists who don't want to pay to enter the resort.

On the approach to the entrance gate next to the three flagpoles and the 'Quartier Naturiste du Cap d'Agde' sign is a car wash. Look carefully to see a footpath that leads into the Réserve Naturelle du Bagnas (the same area of land that starts at the dunes behind the swingers beach). The late afternoon is the best time to take a stroll down this path if you are hoping to do more than just give the dog a good walk. Although not as frequented as the various spots in the nudist resort (remember that we are now in textile territory), you should nevertheless find one or two willing spectators on most days.

Just off the beaten path are several thickets of vegetation with clearings which, if they haven't been manmade, are nature's invitation to be naughty. The other recognised place for exhibitionism just outside the resort is in the car park at La Roquille Beach, the clothed beach on the other side of Port Ambonne (for directions, see the map on page 168).

Jimmy, a streetwise voyeur from nearby Mèze (France), explains how couples should go about indicating their desire to show off. 'A couple drives by once to check out who's around. Then they drive by again but this time the woman in the passenger seat has pulled up her skirt a bit higher than it was before. If they drive by a third time, expect the skirt to be around the waist. Then they should stop the car.' Like all codes of this nature, nothing is set in stone. Even so, these suggestions give novice exhibitionists useful pointers when venturing out to look for voyeurs rather than have them come to you in droves inside the nudist resort.

Always cover up before going in

Be mindful of the risks of catching and transmitting the HIV virus (which causes AIDS) and other sexually transmitted diseases (STDs) when having sexual relations with other people.

You would have though that in a place such as Cap d'Agde this concern would be a burning issue, but it seems not. You rarely hear people talk about sexual health issues around the resort, which can mean one of two things: either people use protection as a matter of course, making such talk academic, or they don't want to be party poopers by raising this heavy subject, whether they use protection or not.

Condoms are used in most places most of the time, according to many regulars. You will usually find a basket of condoms at the entrance to the playrooms in the swingers clubs, most guests at private parties come prepared, and the small fluorescent canisters you see hanging from peoples' necks on the swingers beach are not only for keeping cigarettes dry. Even so, you will still find **Couples Contre le Sida** (Couples Against AIDS), a French organisation concerned with AIDS prevention for swinging couples, on the swingers beach and around the resort for a few weeks during high season.

Some people are shocked by what they consider to be a blasé attitude to using condoms. 'I'd meet plenty of blokes who wanted to fuck me,' says Helen, a gang-bang specialist from Croydon (U.K.), 'but when I asked them if they had a condom, they'd look at me blankly and shrug their shoulders. It wasn't the language barrier—they just didn't seem to care if they wore one or not.' And occasionally you'll hear more disturbing stories of teenage girls having anal sex on the beach with a complete stranger who is not wearing a condom. Such occurrences are the exception rather than the rule, but these stories do show that the responsibility for AIDS prevention in Cap d'Agde, as elsewhere, rests with each visitor.

More authoritative places than this guide exist for information about AIDS, other STDs, and the best way in which to prevent them. Protecting yourself from HIV and other STDs is all about avoiding contact between contaminating body fluids and the body's entry points for these infectious agents. For HIV, contaminating body fluids include: blood, male and female sexual secretions (sperm, vaginal secretions, and to a lesser extent the seminal fluid leaked before ejaculation), and maternal milk. (Saliva does not contain the virus in sufficient quantities to cause contamination.) The key entry points for the virus are as follows: vaginal wall, cervix, uterus, gland of the penis, urethra, rectum, and lesions in the skin or mouth.

Plenty of exciting and sexually stimulating group activities do not require protection from HIV or other STDs. The following are some ideas:

- Sensual massages
- Erotic baths and showers
- Masturbating side-by-side in a group
- Stripteases
- Watching porn films
- Role-playing games
- BDSM

For more information, contact Couples Contre le Sida (Couples Against Aids), 21 Place Tolozan, 69001 Lyon, France (04 72 00 87 36; www.ccsida.com; ccs@ccsida.com).

Chapter 5

The Loner

Unlike many other swingers resorts and even naturist centres in the world, nothing stops single men from visiting Cap d'Agde. Their money will be taken happily by the rental agencies, restaurants, bars, and shops, and they constitute a sizeable part of the Cap's population. The extent to which they will be made to feel at home (or ostracised) depends on several factors, not all of which are in their control. Singles coming to Cap d'Agde primarily for the sex—which has to be the majority—should be forewarned that attitudes towards them will sometimes be ambivalent.

In recent years, relations between the genuine swinging singles and the couples upon whom they usually depend for their fun have been strained by the irresponsible actions of people who have little interest in 'the lifestyle' as such, who come to Cap d'Agde because they have read or seen on TV that here you can fuck anything that moves. When they arrive in what they believe to be the world's biggest (and only!) free brothel, they act as if they have a God-given right to satisfy themselves. Seduction, class, humour, and, most seriously, respect are missing. And when these men are inevitably turned down they have a tantrum. Not surprising, then, that many couples are suspicious of single men.

Unfortunately, the nice guy who has come to the Cap to sample its famed open-mindedness and tolerance may feel rejected by many simply because he is alone. The good news is that many couples come to Cap d'Agde not only to meet other couples but also single guys. These couples are as disappointed as you in the behaviour of the few and are just waiting for that Prince Charming with the 8-inch dick to sweep them off their feet. If you have thick enough skin to weather the occasionally frosty first contact, you will have the opportunity to let your amazing personality shine through and win the day.

For single women, the problem is not so much how to overcome the suspicion and be popular as how to keep the randy hordes at bay (see *Notes for a Single Woman* on page 158).

How to be a successful swinging single

Just as single men have been categorised by some couples as pushy, unrefined, and, quite frankly, a pain in the arse, guys also tend to see couples who choose to spend their holidays at a place well known for its easy-going attitude to sex as gagging for it. Loners have the initial impression that little effort is required to get laid. Wrong!

The first rule of being a successful swinging single is to forget the fact that Cap d'Agde is a nudist resort and that many of its nudists also are libertines. All this description means is that you are mixing with like-minded people, just as you would be if you went on a golfing holiday or an educational cruise of the Greek islands. And just as you would hardly assume that 'X' was dying to suck you off on the 18th green and that 'Y' longed for you to take her on the crumbled ruins of a Greek temple, you have no reason to think or act differently here.

The single guys who have the most fun in Cap d'Agde are those who think of packing their charm before the condoms. Sure, some couples want a quick, physical liaison with little foreplay in the verbal—and sometimes even the physical—sense, but the vast majority of couples and single woman expect to be wooed and seduced before they consider playing with you.

The pot of gold at the end of the rainbow

What sets Cap d'Agde apart from the golfing holiday, the educational cruise of the Greek islands (take a huge sigh of relief, for there *is* a difference), and other conventional dating scenarios is that, once you have scored, people become the lust-seekers you always knew they were and sexual taboos are few and far between. Frustrated after having plied your date with fine wines and expensive Belgian chocolates only to discover that she doesn't like giving head? In Cap d'Agde, she also might not like giving head—to less than five men at a time. So, what lies in store for the swinging single who plays his cards right?

One-on-one sex with no one watching. Swinging couples hardly find much point in one half of the couple going behind the back of the other to sleep with a guy if they are both happy sleeping around together. For this reason, having affairs with cheating wives is not what the Cap is all about. However, picking up a single woman and having a holiday romance like anywhere else is possible.

And sometimes you will have one-on-one sex with a Cap d'Agde-esque twist. 'One day I met a couple on the beach,' says Steve from Sydney (Australia). 'The husband was a grey-haired old man who must have been over 70, while the wife was much, much younger. It looked like a classic case of the husband who was no longer able to satisfy the wife but got off watching her with younger guys. So I went round to their apartment that night ready to put on quite a show. But when I arrived it didn't seem that the old guy was very interested in my presence. As I played around with his wife he'd be washing the dishes, and while we were going at it like rabbits in the bedroom I'd hear him laughing at some TV show.'

And if you think that story is slightly off-putting, spare a thought for Cristoforo from Florence (Italy). 'I was on the bed making love to the wife when the husband pulled back the sheets, got in, rolled over, and went to sleep, right next to where we were having sex. He even started to snore.'

One-on-one sex with someone watching. Don't underestimate the number of husbands who are hugely turned on watching their wives have sex with a complete stranger. You will be required to do no more than have fun with one half of the couple as the other simply watches. Photographs and movies could also be part of the deal, but you will naturally have to discuss such issues before the games commence.

Your main challenge will be forgetting that you have company, which can impede an erection. 'I thought it was my lucky day when a guy asked if I would like to fuck his Asian girlfriend,' says Phillipe from Toulouse (France). 'But when it came down to it I just couldn't get hard. The girl was very hot but this guy wouldn't stop smoking his pipe. I knew he was there—I could smell him—and in the end it ruined everything.'

MMF threesome. Arguably the most common sex a single man will have in Cap d'Agde is a threesome involving two men (him and the male half of the couple) and one woman (the female half of the couple). The couple's motivation for searching for this type of experience could be to satisfy the voyeuristic tendencies of the male partner or some other sexual practice enjoyed by either or both of them. For instance, the woman may like to be pleasured by two men—and in some cases you will be called on to perform one of the more tricky manoeuvres in a sexual repertoire: the double penetration or DP. This one is not for novices still acclimatising to group sex—and nerves could have an adverse effect on your ability to produce an erection. If you have been assigned the tighter passageway, you will need to be as straight as a post. No one said that being a stud was easy.

Another fantasy of couples who indulge in MMF threesomes, and one which people are becoming less and less shy about realising in these sexually emancipated times, is when everyone plays with everyone. The problem as far as heterosexual single men are concerned is that couples do not always explain at the outset that they are looking for a bisexual third person.

This agenda is a potential source of embarrassment, as Claudio from Lugano (Switzerland) can testify. 'I was having a good sixty-nine with Jane [name changed] while John [name changed] was kissing Jane's neck. But when I opened my eyes and looked down I saw it was Jane that was kissing John's neck, even though I still felt someone sucking me. I said to Jane the next day on the beach that I was not bisexual. "Nor is John," she said. "I don't know what got into him."'

But just as couples sometimes keep their bisexuality quiet in the hope that you get carried away in the heat of the moment, straight single men also have a habit of saying that they are bisexual just to get invited to play with a couple. Either way, more openness and honesty is called for.

MFF threesome. Those coming to Cap d'Agde in search of the Holy Grail of male sexual fantasies—sex with two women at the same time—will have their work cut out. Much easier to find when you are operating as a couple (one of the two men in a foursome might just prefer to watch, allowing the other to effectively have a threesome with the two women), a single man will have to find not just one but two women in a place where the fairer sex are in high demand. Having said this, lucky sods such as Dev from London will give hope to dreamers everywhere: 'Enjoying a mother and her daughter at the same time is not unheard of. I had one on each end and then they switched,' he says.

Gang-bang. A gang-bang is where a group of men (more than two) have sex with a single woman. A lot of the time, especially on the swingers beach and other public places, what starts as a threesome develops into a gang-bang when other single men see what's going on and gather round for a piece of the action.

'I followed a couple who were flirting with me on the beach into the dunes,' says Neil from Chessington (U.K.). 'They led me to what we thought was a secluded spot, and I started to touch the woman. I don't know where they came from, but in a few seconds there were about 10 other men huddled round us.' In such situations the sex will be quick and unceremonious, and the woman's enjoyment presumably derives as much from the quantity as the quality of her lovers.

As with a lot of other lifestyle activities, the woman often bends over backwards (sometimes literally) to please her partner. In gang-bang situations the husband will be the ringmaster, saying who can and cannot participate. Also don't be surprised if he gives you instructions while you are in the act: 'faster', 'slower', 'she likes it like that', 'cum on her tits'. Although such interjections may prove to be off-putting, how reassuring it is to meet couples who know each other's sexual preferences inside and out.

Blessed are the meek, respectful and devilishly good-looking, for they shall inherit the Earth

No magic formula exists for getting laid—not even in Cap d'Agde. For every couple who likes a well-endowed stud, another values intelligent conversation more than the size of someone's sexual apparatus. And although some couples go for the confidant, cocky men, just as many are drawn to the strong, silent types. But desperation always turns people off. Keeping the libido in check *is* difficult when all around you are naked people thinking about sex, talking about sex, and having sex. Even so, do your best not to let this libido hang out so much that it makes you seem like a sex maniac.

Spend a day or two on the swingers beach observing how some of the competition operates, and you will quickly appreciate the value of reserve and tact. Rarely do you see the type of men who flit from one couple to the next proposing their sexual services actually going home with any of these people— no matter how handsome and naturally gifted they are. At the end of the day, when the beach has thinned out and only the stragglers are left, these desperados will be milling around lamenting how frigid people are these days and harping back to the good old days when the Cap was one big orgy.

They are in denial. They have dragged their desperation

around like a ball and chain. This is not to say that if you lay your towel down in the middle of the beach, put on your sunglasses and personal stereo, and don't look at anyone all day, couples will be queuing up to play with you. You must flirt to a certain extent, but remaining calm, confident, and ever-so-slightly indifferent also is a good strategy.

Remember to show respect in everything you say and do as a swinging single in Cap d'Agde. Here's an example of the desperados a little earlier in the day as they are overheard talking about their favourite subject: sex. The conversation goes like this:

'Hey, Pascal, you see that one over there?'

'Yeah.'

'Well, I did her the other day.'

'Oh yeah, what was she like?'

'A real slut. She loved every minute of it.'

'Don't you mean every second.'

'You cheeky bastard!' There is a playful scuffle followed by a two-minute silence, during which they stand around fiddling with their dicks.

'Hey, Guy, you see that one over there?'

'Yeah.'

'Well she sucked me off in the dunes this morning.'

'No fucking way! How d'ya manage that.'

'How d'ya think I managed it?' Pascal points down at his four-and-a-half-inch penis and they both grin. They spend the next five minutes whistling at any women who has the courage to pass them on their way to the ice cream cart, greeting other desperados with a Mason-like knock of clenched fists, and, of course, fiddling with their dicks.

'Hey, Pascal, fancy going to the Melrose tonight.'

'Can't. I've got a private party invite.'

'How d'ya manage—' Pascal points to his private parts before Guy can finish the sentence.

'Well, me neither. It's crap at the Melrose anyway. You can't even feel up the women anymore. I'll go get me some action at the sauna.' Five hours later both Pascal and Guy are at home in their pyjamas watching TV with their mothers.

Single men with no manners and no respect deserve to be given short shrift by couples, but they can cut a tragic figure and some people feel sorry for them. Isabelle from Lyon (France) got to know one of the regulars on the swingers beach known as *Gros Bite* (Big Dick). 'He'd been coming here every day for years and was very popular with the other local guys because his large penis attracted couples. Anyway that's what he told me. One day he said that he wouldn't be back next year because he was sad that people only used him for his penis. When he said this he was masturbating himself, so I thought he wasn't serious. But next year he wasn't there, and I've never seen him again.'

Respect in the swinging context does not necessarily mean kissing the feet of the couple you are interested in (unless you have a foot fetish). Nor does it mean not speaking until you are spoken to. Just act like a human being interacting normally with another human being. If the couple then wants to be treated like a piece of meat once they have dragged you back to their apartment, then is the time to let fly with the dirty pillow talk. And remember that couples talk to other couples about the single men they meet. If you have been cool and respectful with couple A, even if there has been no chemistry, you might be recommended to couple B, C, D, and so on.

You could follow all of the rules for being a successful swinging single only to be passed over for someone who, basically, is just better looking than you. Yet another indication that the ground rules for getting laid in Cap d'Agde are no different from anywhere else.

Happy hunting

Assuming you are armed with the good qualities mentioned above, you have, broadly speaking, three hunting grounds in Cap d'Agde: on the beach during the day; on the beach and elsewhere around the resort at night; and inside the bars and clubs. All are teaming with potential prey, but don't expect to be the only one hunting.

'What makes the Cap so special for me is that everywhere I go I feel as though something could happen,' says Tore from Oslo (Norway). 'On some trips I don't do anything sexual at all, but I leave feeling exhausted. The tension is all around, and this can be very exciting.'

A lot of sand—but no desert

The swingers beach is the most obvious place for single men to find partners for sex. A paradise for exhibitionists and voyeurs, this place also is for those who like to touch—be it in full view of their fellow sunbathers or somewhere more private. Unfortunately, no rule exists for identifying the couples who could be looking for an extra guy.

Some men swear that they have a better chance the further back towards the dunes they are. So, on a sweltering hot day when anyone in their right mind wants to be as close to the sea and its cooling breezes as possible, you will always find a resilient group of men sweating at the back of the beach in the hope that interested couples will approach them. Although this spot is a good place to monitor the people entering the dunes for possible action, no real evidence suggests that you will pick up couples easier here than in any other position on the beach. Besides which, how much fun can it be spending the whole day swatting flies and mopping your brow? Being among the fray where at least you have a better chance of talking to people is better.

One possible tip, again hit-and-miss, for identifying a couple with whom you might stand a chance is to target those where the man is considerably older than the woman. The logic behind such a tactic is that:

- Such couples could have difficulty attracting other couples if one of the four is much older than the others.
- The man might be more interested in watching his partner have sex with a stranger than taking part himself.

Such was the case when Metje and Philip from Maastricht (Holland) took a pretty young blonde from the Côte d'Azur and her sugar daddy husband down to the play-rooms at Le Glamour. 'I agreed to it to please Philip,' Metje admits. 'The other guy was old enough to be my father—and I'm in my forties.'

'Anyway, in the end it didn't matter,' says Philip. 'The old guy couldn't get it up.'

'He said he liked me and everything but what really turned him on was watching his wife with other men. So he spent the rest of the time masturbating while we had a three-some,' adds Metje.

'And that was cool!' says Philip, smiling.

So, how do you score on the swingers beach? Don't for-get the importance of eye contact—as opposed to merely look-ing at someone while wearing sunglasses. No one can tell if you are looking at them or just in their general direction, so remove the shades to leave no doubt.

Also, don't underestimate the sexual power of humour. This suggestion is not to say that you should come to the Cap with an arsenal of your dirtiest jokes translated into French, or even that you should go out of your way to be a bubbly, jovial person if your personality is naturally more sedate. But remember to *smile* every now and again, espe-cially at the people with whom you are flirting. Eye contact and smiling: hardly ground-breaking revelations in the 'how to get laid' debate, but rest assured they will be as effective on the swingers beach in Cap d'Agde as anywhere else.

On the prowl at night

Flirting on the beach is all very well, but even in its rather special Cap d'Agde context it can be a rather clichéd activ-ity—fun and productive, but clichéd nonetheless. You are hardly going to amaze friends back home with stories of how you met such and such a person on the beach during your summer holiday at one of the largest beach resorts in France. What will impress them, however, are the anecdotes about

146

how you went out at night and took part in a gang-bang in the car park, the transvestite giving multiple blow jobs on a moonlit beach, and the time when you were walking home one evening when a couple drove by and asked if you would like to join them for a threesome.

The stuff wet dreams are made of? Perhaps. But in Cap d'Agde, even today, these activities still happen. You only have to look at the number of local men who come to the resort night after night to walk, wait, and watch in the hope of finding what they are evidentially lacking at home. Along with the goings-on at the swingers beach, the alternative Cap d'Agde nightlife (that which takes place outside the bars and clubs) is largely misunderstood and misrepresented.

As is the case with the swingers beach, what goes on nowadays after dark in the resort is radically different to what went on when the security was less strict. At that time, by all accounts, it was a veritable playground. 'Remember what the jetty was like, Tony?' says Nathalie from Clermont-Ferrand (France), who first started coming to Cap d'Agde in the late 1980s. 'It was a procession of all the perverted souls in this nasty place, that's what is was like,' replies her friend from Oxford (U.K.)—approvingly or disapprovingly it's hard to say. 'No matter what you were looking for—men, couples, voyeurs— you'd find it walking up and down the jetty after dark.'

'No one goes there anymore, though. It's not the same,' says Nathalie. Fences and other barriers have been put up in Port Nature Village, making access to the jetty more difficult. The risk of the police arriving unannounced also is a deterrent, as it is virtually everywhere else. Police cars can be seen patrolling the car parks at night, and some of the regular night prowlers also claim that officers dressed in civvies have now even infiltrated their ranks.

Yet despite the fact that Big Brother is definitely watching, sex under the *belle étoile* continues—less openly than before, but continues nonetheless. Take Edwidge and Pierre from Orléans (France) and Benoit from Nice (France), for

Some of the wine labels in Cap d'Agde make the buyer not care about the quality of the wine. Although the wine in this region of France is not as good as other regions, it's palatable and can be inexpensive. PHOTO: Mark Ashworth

example, who met one pleasant July evening near the port. Looking for a quieter spot to play, they end up in the bushes next to the car park by the now defunct open-air cinema. Edwidge kneels down and starts to suck the two men when a municipal police pickup truck enters the car park. The three libertines hit the deck like Vietnam veterans. They remain on their bellies, hearts pounding as fast as their libidos, until the danger has passed. Then they all get up and continue as if nothing had happened. Irrepressible Human Nature 1, Mean Sex Police 0.

Swinging singles interested in sampling this side of the Cap d'Agde nightlife need to know where to go and what to do when they get there. Over the years, certain places in the resort have become known by couples and singles alike as meeting places for what British swingers describe as 'dogging' (a term used to cover outdoor exhibitionism or sex in public places). The main ones are as follows (to situate them, consult the map on page 44):

The beach. As lively as the swingers beach and dunes

are during the day, they are more or less completely gay after dark, as is the stretch of beach and dunes that runs parallel to the campsite, although here you have a better chance of finding the odd couple every now and then. Wait at the entrance to the beach between Héliopolis and the campsite to monitor who goes down onto the beach. You can assume that those who do are probably up for something kinky, unless they arrive with dogs, children, or metal detectors. Use your common sense and, given the heightened security risk at night, a certain amount of caution when deciding whether to flirt with a potential target.

The jetty. As has been mentioned previously, the jetty at the end of the channel that connects Port Ambonne to the open sea was the meeting place par excellence for libertines after dark. The jetty was a popular play spot because it is isolated, sufficiently lit by the beacon at its end, and by the sea. Although the days of silent processions of pleasure-seekers are past, you will still occasionally find some group sex taking place on the beach next to the jetty, in the bushes on the channel path, and even in small boats anchored close by.

Car parks. A secluded car park is one of the most popular locations for dogging. The resort has plenty, and you would do well to include them on your nightly tour. Typically sombre with sufficient places to conceal yourself from unwanted attention, the car parks in the Cap have great potential for sex games.

Even so, some car parks are better than others. The one next to the resort's entrance gate by the disused open-air cinema is the best since it backs onto the Réserve Naturelle du Bagnas, which increases the play area to include an expanse of tress, bushes, and other natural hiding places. The car park on the Port Ambonne-side of the entrance gate is less convenient, being next to the office where the private security guards drink coffee and feed their rottweilers.

Likewise, although the car park at Le Glamour would be an ideal place to go to meet excited swingers as they file out of the club at around 02.00, the presence of an attendant makes doing anything provocative difficult. Elsewhere, the car parks around Héliopolis and Port Nature also are worth checking out.

Port Nature. The path that runs the length of Port Nature, starting at one end of Testosterone Corridor in Port Nature 5 and ending at the beach in Port Nature 1, is one of the resort's busiest thoroughfares for pedestrians. The single men have not let this opportunity go to waste, and you invariably see plenty of them skulking around the stairwells leading up to the apartments and walking endlessly up and down the path trying to catch the eye of interested couples. Port Nature Village (the villas on the other side of the path) were once part of the beat, but have become less frequented with the appearance of fences and barriers prohibiting access to all but occupants of the villas themselves.

Hélio Village. Being more secluded and unimpeded by barriers and the like, Hélio Village is a more favoured hunting ground. The maze of paths and alleyways, the darkness, the trees and bushes, and the villas with their open terraces are all perfect for dogging. Note, however, that you risk causing offence by following all and sundry as they innocently return to their villas at night. Some might be interested in playing; but the vast majority will not. Therefore, if you chose to concentrate your efforts here, be extremely tactful.

Outside Le Glamour. Think of dogs waiting for leftovers when visualising the men standing vigil outside Le Glamour towards closing time at 02.00. They wait in front of the club on the sandy track that runs parallel to the beach and proposition couples leaving the club. As opportunistic as this tactic may sound, it can sometimes be successful.

The logic is hard to resist. You stand outside a club infamous for its hype. A couple leaves, frustrated (at least as far as the husband is concerned) that they have not done what they had hoped to do inside. They are approached by a guy who doesn't look too bad in the dark. He asks whether a

threesome would be of interest. The couple would have pre-
ferred another couple, but at this late stage in the evening
beggars can't be choosers. So they agree. The same logic
applies to standing outside the other swingers clubs in the
resort, although none of them has as convenient a waiting
area as the sandy track in front of Le Glamour.

Night prowling etiquette

Knowing where to go to find sex after dark in Cap d'Agde is
only half the story; you must also be *au fait* with night prowling etiquette. Night prowling is not for the shy and retiring
types. Success depends on your ability to be forward and as-
sertive without being overly pushy and, ultimately, creepy. Although flirting in a bar typically starts with eye contact, in
most of the public places mentioned above you will show your
interest in a particular couple by following them. This does not
mean that you should stalk them—though admittedly the line
between the two is sometimes difficult to draw. If, for instance,
you see a couple leave Le Glamour at 02.00 and they go down
onto the beach, turning all the while to see who's behind them,
you could reasonably assume they want to be followed. Likewise, when a husband, knowing you are in hot pursuit, pulls
up his wife's skirt and slaps her buttocks, you know your presence is not unwelcome.

When you are less certain whether the couple you are
following wants to play, keep a respectful distance and be
receptive to the slightest hint that you should get lost. A
quickened walk; huffs, puffs, and groans; and the brandishing of mobile phones to call the police are all strong indica-
tions you should give up the chase. Use common sense when
selecting your targets. The woman in slippers, curlers, and
a hairnet who has just slipped outside for a cigarette before
bed is not a prime candidate for a steamy night of outdoor
sex—however mouth-watering the image.

You also should know when to let go. Some men keep
couples under surveillance for half the night, occasionally even
following them to the door of their apartments. 'If it's left open,

we can enter,' says one anonymous local prowler. For every couple who leaves the door open there will be hundreds who will close it, bolt it, and push a chair up against it. Why not ask a couple before they go up to their apartment whether they would like your company? That said, why not ask the same question before you start to follow them? Such directness is often appreciated more than the subsequent game of cat-and-mouse, you minimise the risk of offending people, and you will save wear and tear on your feet.

Drinking from the source

As difficult as it is nowadays to avoid the security and actually find willing partners as you roam around the resort at night, bear in mind that the libertines who come to the Cap don't just stop wanting to have sex; instead they change the places where they look for it.

The bars, clubs, and saunas are where the majority of the nocturnal action takes place in the 21st century version of Cap d'Agde, creating a frustrating state of affairs for the swinging single. Most clubs (for a complete listing, see page 116) either prohibit single men altogether or make their entry conditional on strict rules and the payment of a hefty admission fee. And once inside, they have no guarantee that the couples in attendance will be looking for MMF threesomes and that they will even be allowed into the playrooms unless accompanied by someone of the opposite sex.

Even the promising 'gang-bang' and 'trio' nights advertised by some clubs have a habit of turning into an almighty ruck for the one or two females who have bothered to turn up, and you will miss out if you are not in the right place at the right time.

Before you pay your 50 euro or so for what could be an average evening, try your luck at the Melrose Café. Priority is given to couples if the bar is packed, but otherwise all are welcome. You will also notice many of the people milling around in the corridor in front of the bar are single men. They are not waiting patiently for a table, or even because

You wouldn't be in France if you didn't tipple on a drop of *vino* from time to time—and you wouldn't be in Cap d'Agde if you didn't purchase it as God had intended.

they have a burning desire to see their umpteenth strip show. They are, in fact, waiting for couples in what has become one of the most strategically important and productive places in the resort for swinging singles.

Couples sometimes choose their favourite guy on leaving the bar, or make clear by a look or a gesture that they would like to be followed. (Note that some men will follow couples whether they have been encouraged to do so or not. If you decide to do the same, be careful not to offend anyone by being too pushy or tenacious.)

You also could do the unthinkable and enter the bar yourself, buy a drink, and talk to people. No doubt a strategy to favour the brave, but one that proves more rewarding than waiting passively in the hope that tonight will be your lucky night. At the resort's other bar for swingers, the Hemingway Café, you will have no choice but to interact with your potential partners. It has no viewing corridor, and success depends on your ability to make contact with couples either verbally over the loud techno music or on the small dance floor. Hemingway's has fewer couples than the Melrose, although those that do come are arguably more frequently looking for MMF threesomes.

This point is evidenced by the large number of youngish, usually local lads who can be found at the Hemingway on most nights during high season. Not really swinging singles in the strict sense of the word, these boys will often be after anything they can get: a grope of a pair of tits, a sexy smooch with a horny housewife, or a punch-up outside—doesn't really matter to them. Of course these types exist elsewhere in the resort—at the Melrose, on the swingers beach, in the clubs—and they make the task of gaining the confidence of couples that much harder for the genuine lifestyler who happens to be single.

If you have had no success in the bars and you are not taken with the idea of joining the nocturnal wanderers in search of opportunistic sexual encounters, the option of going to a swingers club grows more attractive. Sex, after all, is a drug as strong and addictive as any other. Just as the poker player has convinced himself that his losses will be recouped in the next hand, the horny single guy who has struck out in the bars is now sure that the mysterious sanctum of a swingers club is where all of the action is taking place—and is where he needs to be. Although often this thinking is valid, even here, like everywhere else in Cap d'Agde, you are not 100% sure of getting laid.

The only club that accepts single men at all times is Le Pharaon. Although some nights are devoted officially to gang-bangs and others to threesomes, they all tend to follow the same formula: 10, 15, or even 20 times the number of men than women. You find the same scene at the Nat Hamman, the swingers sauna that welcomes singles, and the Quai des Anges, the club in the nearby town of Agde that specialises in gang-bangs. You don't have to be an economist to work out how your prospects will be affected by such an inequality of supply and demand.

You can have a lot of fun at these places, but realise from the outset that in most cases you must be prepared to share the couples you meet. Ideally you will want to find a single woman to accompany you to a club reserved for couples, where there will be a greater balance in the number of boys and girls present.

Don't assume that the doors at these places will be flung wide open to welcome you just because you are coming in with another couple. More often than not you won't be allowed in, especially during high season. Then again, depending on your and your friends' powers of persuasion and the humour of the doorman at the time, you might be lucky. The edge comes off this achievement, though, when you must pay about twice as much as the couple you are with. By the way, Monday nights at Le Glamour are open to single men.

Catching the rare *singlus womanus*

In many ways, you have struck the jackpot if you manage to hitch up with a single woman while in Cap d'Agde. For a start, they are notoriously thin on the ground. The good news when you do finally see a nice-looking one is that she will probably not be a hooker (prostitution is rare and widely frowned on in the Cap). But odds are that she's there to work in one of the bars, clubs, or restaurants rather than play. Either that or she, also, will be looking for other girls. So, assuming that you have found someone who has come to Cap d'Agde to party—with men rather than women—you now have to win her amid the fierce competition from other single men.

No one said that the search for the Holy Grail would be easy, but once found and firmly in your grasp, it can be the source of much pleasure: a holiday romance or a dirty week-end, with previously closed doors flung wide open as you start to operate as a couple. With a woman at your side there is no restriction to the number of swingers clubs you can visit, and you will find meeting other people easier with a female in tow. And who knows, you might even like the person. 'I met Françoise on the swingers beach,' recalls Ross from Montréal (Canada). 'Six weeks later she was one of the most important people in my life.'

Meeting a single woman adds to your Cap d'Agde experience. But where are the best places to go looking for them? For starters, stop making a beeline for the swingers beach each morning. Single women, even if they are libertines, are rarely seen there. This situation is rather like the girl who enjoys one-night stands but thinks that she should not. 'It's the first time I've done this,' she'll say, as she drags you back to her place. She needs to go through the motions of making a symbolic gesture that she is in fact a respectable woman. And respectability in Cap d'Agde is sunbathing among the wrinkled naturists and screaming children on the family beach.

Take a stroll along the beach, starting at the jetty, to check out the talent. Plenty of the women will be unavailable. They could have partners back at the apartment sleeping off the previous night's excesses; their husbands could be playing in the sea with the kids; or they themselves might also be kids, despite looking older from a distance.

An especially good place to find the more beautiful women is at the two points along the beach—opposite the restaurant L'Horizon and the Espace Villa Romaine—where deck chairs are available for rent. Perhaps the single women see this space as a sanctuary, offering a limited protection from gazing eyes. Alternatively, given the relative expense of renting a deck chair in Cap d'Agde, women could be weeding the rich suitors from the poor. The same arguments apply at the resort's swimming pools, which also are good places to look for single women.

At night, the resort fills with locals. Of these, a reasonable proportion will be women. Find them at the Melrose and the Hemingway. The oyster bar at the Espace Villa Romaine next to the entrance to Le Glamour also is a good spot to look for women who wouldn't mind accompanying you (getting you into) a swingers club.

If all else fails and you have not found a date, try convincing the doormen at the resort's gay swingers club, La Scala, that you are really a lover of men rather than women. Once inside, you will invariably find a gaggle of heterosexual women who have come to this club precisely to avoid the likes of you. At least you will have a captive audience—whose guard will most probably be down—on which to work your charm.

The world's biggest drive-in: The voyeur

As is the case at naturist centres the world over, a considerable part of the male population comes to Cap d'Agde to do no more than look. This mission is especially true for Cap d'Agde, which, unlike conventional nudist resorts, has mixed nudity with sex. The resulting cocktail is a voyeur's delight. For a description of the places in the resort to go for good shows, as well as some pointers on etiquette and code, see *For Their Eyes Only: The Exhibitionist* on page 130.

You must still conduct yourself well, showing respect for others, and be careful to avoid the police and security when and where applicable—especially if you are the type of voyeur who likes to show his appreciation of a good show by giving a masturbatory round of applause. But, unlike the swinging single, you will rarely feel as though you are banging your head against a brick wall to find what you came for. Something sexy and erotic is always available for voyeurs in Cap d'Agde; touching and playing is a different ballgame altogether.

Notes for a single woman

Harping on about where single women should go to get laid in Cap d'Agde would be rather like giving the same advice to a guy in a brothel. In many ways, given the relative scarcity of single women in the resort and the perpetually high demand for them among single males, couples, and even other women, the advice should perhaps be how to *avoid* having—or at least being asked to have—sex. Women who come to the Cap for the naturism rather than for anything sexual may especially need this information.

Many men perceive all single women as fair game. The women who come to Cap d'Agde with even a slightly prudish attitude run the risk of feeling more like objects than human beings.

On the other hand, rarely will you feel as important and have as much power as you will in Cap d'Agde. You hold all the cards; the secret to having a great holiday is knowing how to play them. If you are open-minded and a bit of a flirt, you can find what you like—be it romantic evenings or raunchy sex. The following are a few of the benefits you will enjoy while in Cap d'Agde, and tips on how to take every advantage of them:

Popularity. Even if they aren't always so interested in your sparkling wit, tales of travel, and abiding love of world peace, you'll have the opportunity to meet as many people as you want to meet during your holiday in Cap d'Agde. The vast majority of them will only want to get into your pants. Even couples are often looking for an extra girl to act out the paradigm of male fantasies, the MFF threesome, or for a quality moment of sapphic love. Although some will be heavy-handed in their approach, others will be charming, even seductive.

This description sounds like your average Saturday night at the local disco, doesn't it? Only in Cap d'Agde the encounters tend to be a lot less one-dimensional. Although sex is the starting point, deeper relationships and even lasting friendships can develop. Single girls who want the most from their holiday will take their popularity, forget the carnal desires that motivate it, and use it to their own ends. If you fancy the person or people who approach you, that's fine. Go home with them and indulge yourself.

If, on the other hand, you find them interesting people without being sexually attractive, you must lead them down a different path. Explain upfront that you just want to be friends and see what happens. You might be surprised that in a place where everyone seems to think and act with their genitalia just how platonic relationships can be.

The pick of the crop. Single women in Cap d'Agde can expect high quality as well as quantity. Not all of your suitors will be sexy hunks—far from it. But you can act safe in the knowledge that if you pass up the above-average-but-slightly-podgy André, the drop-dead-gorgeous Rodrigo will not be too long in coming.

And you can be as shallow as the people who are trying get into your pants when selecting partners. One day a man was sheltering from the rain in his car next to the Buvette de Marseillan. He thought he saw a woman he knew, so he invited her into his car. When she got in, he saw that he had made a mistake and didn't know her. But no problem—he asked if she would have sex with him anyway. She looked at his penis and manually inspected it before saying yes.

Cap d'Agde is a buyer's market for women, and as such you should not feel pressure to settle for anything but the best. Forget hypnotherapy, self-help books, and several coats of makeup; come to Cap d'Agde for an instant confidence booster.

Free nights out. Single women rarely have to pay an admission fee when visiting a swingers club; moreover, occasionally they are even given free drinks. And what are you expected to do in return? Just sit around looking pretty. The management and other customers would be more than happy if you headed straight for the playrooms, but women have absolutely no obligation to do anything sexual.

You must respect the club's dress code, so don't turn up wearing jeans and flip-flops, but otherwise you can spend the whole time just drinking and dancing if you so choose (the same applies at the sauna, where you can use the facilities without any obligation to have sex). Your mere presence is enough.

As a single women, you'll find no shortage of people dying to invite you to visit a club with them. Here, again, your admission will be taken care of, as no doubt will your drinks. But establish the ground rules of such a visit before you enter the club. If you have no intention of swinging, make this intent clear at the outset. By the same token, don't be offended if your date, once he has used you for entrance, goes AWOL for most of the evening. Discuss both parties' expectations in advance. Being used in such situations is no big deal provided that everyone knows for what they are being used.

Chapter 6

The Gay

Just when you thought that this town was not big enough for the naturists and the libertines, along come the gays to confuse the Cap's already muddled personality. Add to gays the sizeable floating population of single men who, if they aren't completely gay, are certainly open to a quickie in the bushes with another guy, and homosexual games at Cap d'Agde are almost as common as heterosexual ones.

Gays—and to a lesser extent lesbians—have been fatally drawn to the Cap, not so much for its gay-oriented facilities (which to be honest are better in nearby Montpellier), but for its open-minded attitude and renowned tolerance. This section of the Cap's eclectic population is more than merely tolerated. They have become integral to the resort's atmosphere and vibe. Cap d'Agde is neither homophobic nor gay-friendly: it simply doesn't see the point of distinguishing gay from straight. Sex is sex, holes are holes, and provided that you are prepared to live and let live, who really cares what sex goes in what hole?

The gay guide

The dunes are affectionately known in gay circles as *Le Petit Bois Joli* (The Pretty Little Wood), and this place is the hunting ground par excellence of horny males after males. Jean-Christophe from Montpellier (France) remembers that '20 years ago *Le Petit Bois Joli* was almost all gay. There were a few couples but even then most of the men were after men.'

Not much has changed. Most of the activity in the dunes today is gay—at least the section of the dunes (about two-thirds of it) that stretches from the end of the swingers beach to where the nudist beach ends altogether. This stretch of sand is considered to be the gay beach, and although perhaps not as crowded as the adjacent swingers beach, its population is no less naughty.

Surprisingly, you'll see little gay exhibitionism on the beach itself. In the dunes, however, almost anything goes, which is especially true at night when the beach and dunes are virtually 100% gay. After dark, spend some time loitering at the entrance to the beach between Héliopolis and the campsite. This completely unremarkable spot is quite unpleasant on windy days, but it is *the* place to find nocturnal action. You will not have to wait too long before a likely lad comes by, making eye contact as he heads down onto the beach. If interested, you are then supposed to follow him to a quiet spot on the sand or all the way to the dunes.

Exercise caution and trust your instincts if something doesn't feel right to avoid things getting any stickier than you had bargained for. Elsewhere in the resort at night, most of what goes on is of the heterosexual variety. In general, though, gays can expect to enjoy as much action as heterosexuals do, sometimes from surprising sources. 'I even had an adventure with a straight guy this summer,' says Arnaud, a 40-something banker from Paris (France). 'He passed in front of my apartment, we looked at each other, he came up to my floor, I invited him into my apartment, and the rest I'll leave to your imagination.'

In the great scheme of things, the Cap doesn't have too many gay-oriented facilities—and fewer seem to re-open every year. In 2002, for instance, the gay sauna went straight and the gay swingers club, Le Cléopâtre, became Le Juls, a mostly hetero club. You can expect these two establishments to continue to attract a fair amount of gay and bisexual customers—Le Juls in particular continues to be a popular hangout for lesbians—although a handful of other places do exist for gays to go for a meal, a drink, a boogie, and a bit of slap and tickle.

Although the Rainbow Flag flutters over **Le Look** (04 67 26 30 42), along with the Melrose the other bar on Testosterone Corridor, this is not your typical gay bar. 'We welcome people of all tendencies,' says Eric, the owner, and judging by the motley collection of muscle tops, nurse's uniforms, spiked bras, sensible shirts, and leather jock straps, his claim seems reasonable. Some would say the atmosphere here is no different from any bar in the resort. But Le Look does have a relaxed friendliness that is sadly lacking at other bars. Come here to hook up with your gay friends; but also choose this bar for a quiet drink in pleasant company, regardless of sexual orientation. Note too that the drinks here are considerably cheaper than at the Melrose; a beer, for example, costs 2,70 euro instead of 5.

The eating place of choice—or at least the restaurant that most openly promotes its gay-friendliness—is **La Grange Gourmande,** covered under *Degustation* on page 60. Another restaurant reviewed elsewhere, the **Casa Nueva** (see page 60), is something of a compromise between the go-go dancers and excited housewives at the Melrose to its right and the leather caps, high stools, and techno music at Le Look to its left. Lesbian owners, refined food, and occasional whipping sessions after last orders are big reasons why gays frequent this place as much as anyone else.

With the transformation of Le Cléopâtre into Le Juls, the only gay swingers club is **La Scala** (04 67 26 19 93) in Port Ambonne. This place starts to get going at around 01.00, when it fills up with the crowd you saw earlier in the evening sipping cocktails at Le Look, chewing on frog's legs at the Casa Nueva, and showing off the latest in slutwear in the fashion shows around the resort—for this club is a popular place for models (many of whom are gay) to finish off the evening.

The interior of the club is small, with a raised dance floor opposite the long bar and comfy chairs in an intimate spot out of the glare of the flashing disco lights. No sex club would be complete without a cage for those who fancy themselves as go-go dancers, and La Scala is no exception. Otherwise, the décor is simple without any particular style. When you enter the club, you can either go directly to the bar and dance floor or check out the small adjoining room with a basket of condoms and gel at its entrance.

The playroom, or backroom to use the proper gay term, is probably as dark and scary as following someone to the dunes at midnight. It can also become incredibly pungent as the night wears on—more so it seems than at the straight swingers clubs—no doubt the result of the cramped conditions and heavy use. The backroom is basically two long boxes with small gaps cut into the sides for entering and exiting the fray. Voyeurs are restricted to the occasional glimpse of bare white buttocks pumping in the darkness, and they will probably not hang around for too long on account of the smell. Hardly the most seductive place in the world, but it certainly serves its purpose.

Entrance to La Scala is cheap in comparison with the Cap's other sex clubs: 10 euro, plus the mandatory purchase of a drink charged at 8 euro (for something alcoholic) or 5 euro (for something soft). Neither does there seem to be any requirement that you enter as a couple.

La Scala is not, in fact, the only sex club for gays in Cap d'Agde. Depending on when you are there, **Le Pharaon** (see page 121) is another option for same-sex swingers. Reports conflict as to exactly when this club is officially gay, but it seems to change its sexual orientation from one season to the next. Whatever its colour when you visit, the chances are that it will be more gay-friendly at the beginning of the season.

Le Yanka (see page 77) also attracts its fair share of gays, yet being pretty much the only normal disco in the resort, it actually attracts all types of people who fancy going somewhere to dance when the bars close.

Chapter 7

Beyond the Cap

Relatively few visitors to the nudist resort in Cap d'Agde think of exploring the surrounding area. Why would you want to waste a day or two of your precious two weeks *au naturel* to walk round the cobbled streets of some old town or another while sweating uncomfortably into your T-shirt and shorts? And after a few days unwinding on the beach, the last thing you want to do is face the French train timetables and rejoin the rat race. These sentiments are understandable, and you should not feel like an uncultured philistine just because you don't feel like budging.

But if one day you can muster enough energy, desire, and courage to throw on the civvies and leave the land of the naked lotus-eaters, you will find several places of interest within easy reach of the resort. The greatest attractions of the region—the famous pink brick buildings, medieval churches, and excellent museums of Toulouse, and the wonderful citadel at Carcassonne, for example—are possibilities for excursions, although they are farther away and require more planning.

Cap d'Agde with clothes on

The most obvious destination for those desirous of escaping the nudist resort for a few hours is the clothed part of Cap d'Agde. It's a half-hour walk from the entrance gate of the nudist resort to the **port** of Cap d'Agde: a pleasant stroll along a path reserved for pedestrians and cyclists (for directions, see the map on page 168). If you don't feel like walking, you can rent bikes at the campsite reception by

Doc from Buffalo, N.Y. (USA) decides the challenge of *toro piscine* is better left to French youth and escapes the ring.

the day (8 euro) or by the week (40 euro).

Other than the port with its fancy yachts (not as opulent as those at, say, Saint-Tropez, but not bad nonetheless), there is not much to Cap d'Agde. Indeed for a town on the Mediterranean coast of France, it is ugly and characterless. Perhaps this appearance stands to reason, since the place only came into being in the early 1960s and was never meant to be more than a beach resort. As such you cannot fault the Cap for its selection of holiday accommodations, tourist-style restaurants, nightclubs, and beach-oriented activities, even if it doesn't offer a lot to actually *see.*

The limited points of cultural interest include the **Musée de l'Ephèbe,** which you will pass as you walk into the centre of Cap d'Agde from the nudist resort. The museum has a collection of Greek and Roman relics, including the Ephèbe d'Agde: a Hellenistic bronze statuette that was formerly kept at the Louvre in Paris. **Fort de Brescou,** which lies just offshore and is accessible by ferry from the port, dates from 1680 and served as a prison—like Marseille's Chateau d'If (made famous by Alexandre Dumas' *The Man in the Iron*

The beat of a drum and the high whine of a flute create part of the tension as water-jousters compete on the Hérault.

Mask). The kids will enjoy **Luna Park,** an amusement park on **Ile des Loisirs,** and the water-based **Aqualand** on the mainland opposite Ile des Loisirs, after the less-than-thrilling entertainment available in the nudist resort itself. A casino on Ile des Loisirs caters to grown-up kids.

You can occasionally see exhibitions of the Sètois tradition of water-jousting (for a fuller explanation of what this involves, see *The Twinkling Lights of Sète* on p. 170) on the canalised part of the Hérault River, which can be jovial entertainment while sitting at one of the riverfront cafés.

Another favourite entertainment not found elsewhere is *toro piscine* (bull pool). Imagine an oval stadium with a sandy floor, 30 French teenagers, a small square swimming pool, and an enraged baby bull that wants to kill the boys. The boys win if they can con the bull into jumping into the pool, which is only possible by having the bull chase them. To escape the bull (which is wearing rubber knobs on the tips of its horns for safety reasons), the youths can jump over the perimeter fence. But sometimes the bull also clears the fence, at which point everyone jumps back into the arena

167

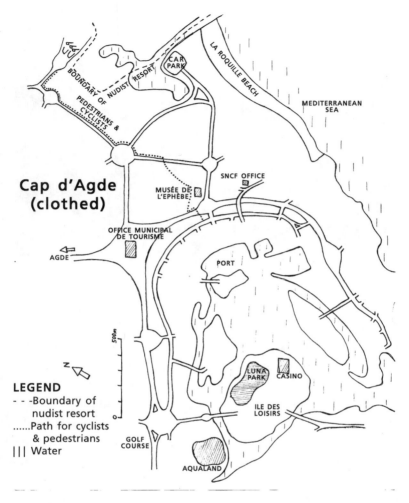

Cap d'Agde (clothed)

MEDITERRANEAN SEA

LA ROQUILLE BEACH

BOUNDARY OF NUDIST RESORT

CAR PARK

BOUNDARY OF PEDESTRIANS & CYCLISTS

SNCF OFFICE

MUSÉE DE L'EPHÈBE

OFFICE MUNICIPAL DE TOURISME

AGDE

PORT

LUNA PARK

CASINO

ILE DES LOISIRS

GOLF COURSE

AQUALAND

500m

N

LEGEND
- - -Boundary of nudist resort
......Path for cyclists & pedestrians
||| Water

Only a part of Cap d'Agde is for naturists. The rest is like any small summer resort town with a water park, casino, and golf course.

for safety. Watching this goofy sport reminds people why young men are sent into battle first.

For more information on these and other attractions in Cap d'Agde, contact the Office Municipal de Tourisme (04 67 01 04 04; contact@capdagde.com).

Caps off to Agde

More interesting than the culturally bankrupt Cap d'Agde is the town of Agde, about 6.5km inland and accessible by bus from the nudist resort. Agde is one of the most unspoilt towns on the Languedocian coast thanks to its position slightly inland. The town is set along the now canalised Hérault River, which connects it to the Mediterranean.

While Cap d'Agde has become overrun with tourists and consumed by the tackiness that seems to follow in their wake, Agde has managed to keep its compact old town quiet and free from development. Take a stroll around the cobbled streets, linked by several *places* that follow the riverside from east to west, for a complete break from the beach resort atmosphere that reigns along the coast.

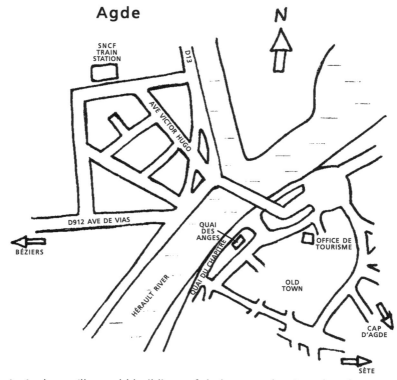

In Agde you'll see old buildings of dark grey volcanic rock rather than the lighter tones of stone used in most old French towns.

The **Musée Agathois** is a decent enough museum featuring exhibits on life in the area from prehistoric times to the present day, and the fortress-like, 12th-century **Saint-Etienne Cathedral** on the south bank of the river is the most impressive of the town's churches. Plan your visit to Agde to coincide with one of the town's market days: Wednesdays and Saturdays for the flea market and Thursdays for produce.

For more information on these and other attractions in Agde, contact the Office de Tourisme (04 67 94 29 68; office-de-tourisme-agde@wanadoo.fr).

The twinkling lights of Sète

Stand on the nudist beach after dark and look to your left down the coast. The lights twinkling enticingly on top of a promontory (called Mont St-Clair) overlooking the sea are those of the pretty town of Sète. Although the town looks close from where you are standing, it is actually 25km from the Cap, making it too far to walk to, a lengthy bike ride, but an easy day trip by car or train. If you are going by car, take the scenic road that winds its way along the coast rather than N112, which follows a more mundane route through the coastal vineyards of this area. Trains leave from the SNCF station in Agde regularly throughout the day and take about 15 minutes to travel to Sète.

Considerably busier than Agde, Sète is nevertheless similar in style: a picturesque town built around a bustling waterway—in Sète's case, it's the **Canal Royal**. Bars, restaurants, and the narrow, winding streets of the **old town** fan out from the west side of the canal, creeping up the side of **Mont St-Clair.** You are likely to spend most of your time either along the canal or exploring the old town.

During summer, competitions of the curious Sètois sport of **water-jousting** take place in the town's canals. The basic idea is the same as land-based jousting, the difference being that here it involves two long boats, each manned by eight oarsman, with the jouster of each vessel standing on a raised platform on the stern. If you miss seeing a live demonstration of the sport, head to the **Musée Paul Valéry,** about a 10-minute walk southwest of Canal Royal, where exhibits are devoted to jousting and the other nautical traditions of the town.

Climb to the summit of Mont St-Clair for **good views** of the town's ports—old and new—and the coastline. In the absence of a promontory and twinkling lights, you will need to use the viewfinders to make out the nudist resort and its naked sunbathers from here. Many unwitting tourists have no doubt dropped in their coins expecting to be regaled with impressive vistas of Mediterranean France, only to have a bunch of bare bottoms and dangly bits invade the lens.

For more information on the various attractions of Sète, contact the Service Tourisme (04 67 74 71 71; tourisme@ville-sete.fr).

Montpellier seems like a metropolis

By far the largest town in these parts is Montpellier, about 60km northeast of Agde. The A9 highway links Agde to Montpellier, and you can also reach the city by catching a train from the SNCF station in Agde. Several trains run each day, and the journey takes about 35 minutes. For those coming to Cap d'Agde by air, Montpellier (or the closer but smaller Béziers) will be your gateway airport. If so, take some time either on arrival or departure to have a look round the city. (The airport is only 8km southeast of the centre and a shuttle bus runs into town.)

Montpellier will seem big in comparison with Cap d'Agde. It has a full range of shops and services, which makes it a good place to stock up on items that are either unavailable or too expensive in the Cap. But Montpellier has even more to offer. It is an attractive, vibrant city, with an interesting mix of classical and avant-garde architecture that is, for the most part, complementary rather than incongruous, combined with a youthful dynamism derived from its university culture.

If the constant sight of far-from-perfect naked bodies (including your own) starts to depress, consider making an excursion to a nearby attraction, such as the beautiful city of Montpellier, to revitalise your senses.

The logical place to begin your tour is **Place de la Comédie,** a five-minute walk north of the SNCF station. You'll see a broad plaza flanked by cafés, the imposing **Opera House,** the city's modernistic tramway, and, just to the north of the plaza at the beginning of **Champs du Mars** park, the tourist office. Halfway up the west side of the park is **Musée Fabré,** which contains an enormous collection of paintings by the likes of Delacroix, Maillol, Zurbáran, and Rubens. Along with this museum, the **old town** is the highlight of Montpellier. Occupying the area to the northwest of Place de la Comédie, these streets are home to some small museums and many elaborate Renaissance mansions worth a day of meandering.

For more information, contact the Office de Tourisme de Montpellier (04 67 60 60 60; contact@ot-montpellier.fr).

The Future?

The greatest achievement of Cap d'Agde and its greatest attraction is the very thing that threatens to bring it all tumbling down. Over the years the resort has managed to become more than just a naturist centre. It is a genuine mix of people from all walks of life, of all sexual persuasions, of all colours, creeds, and classes. It is a true melting pot where you can be exactly what you want to be.

But the acceptance and tolerance for which the Cap is justly famous may be near breaking point. The naturists and libertines haven't been getting on as well as they did in the past. Opinions differ as to whether the Cap is too sexually liberated and needs reeling in. What is indisputable is that today the libertines are on the back foot and fighting to preserve what, for them at least, the Cap is all about.

Some argue that Cap d'Agde should stop trying to be all things to all people and make a decision: is it a swingers resort for adults only or an entirely non-sexual naturist centre for families? That decision might have effectively been taken. The increased security and other measures to clean up the Cap's decadent reputation are only the start of a drive to return the resort to its nudist roots.

Naturists such as Ann and David, who have been living in Cap d'Agde for the past nine years, are upbeat about the future: 'Cap d'Agde has to forge ahead. We have a new, younger mayor who is spending more money on developing the naturist zone. Cap d'Agde as a naturist town has been here for 40 years and will be here as a naturist town for another 40 years.'

But a town needs people; a town needs an economy. The naturists are not filling the resort's restaurants each evening, spending thousands of euro in the shops, and running up large bar tabs. Take the libertines out of Cap d'Agde and most of its businesses would struggle to survive.

The mayor has been spending money on developing facilities, but Cap d'Agde could be like a house of cards if the big spenders fail to turn up. And should the sex policing continue much beyond its current level, those cards could fall. Many libertines say they would not return to the Cap if the screws were tightened any further.

Rumours abound of alternative Cap d'Agdes developing, notably on the Costa Brava in Spain, and time will tell whether the libertines are ready to forsake their spiritual home for pastures new.

Appendix

Schoolboy French Phrasebook

The key to pronouncing French is knowing which letters *not* to pronounce. The following is a selection of the more important general rules of pronunciation:

a   papa

c   s before e, i and y; k before a, o, and u

ç   s

ch shop

é   long a

è   short e

g   vision before e, i and y; god before a, o and u

h   silent

i   sleep

j   vision

ll   yacht

o   cockatoo

qu k

r   try to roll it

s   z between vowels; silent at the end of words

th t

u   like an English long e said with pursed lips

w   usually w; occasionally v (e.g. 'wagon')

x   ks before most consonants; gz before most vowels; silent at the end of words

Now for some basic words and phrases. And remember that adding the honorific of *monsieur, madame,* or *mademoiselle* can be a respectful touch. So instead of just saying 'bonjour' to say hello, say 'bonjour, madame'.

Hello	*bonjour* (day) *bonsoir* (evening)
Goodbye	*au revoir*
Yes	*oui*
No	*non*
Please	*s'il vous plaît*

Thank you	*merci*
My name is...	*je m'appele...*
I am lost	*je suis perdu*
Where is...?	*où est...?*
Do you have...?	*avez-vous...?*
I would like...	*je voudrais...*
I need...	*j'ai besoin de...*
How much?	*c'est combien?*
What time is it?	*quelle heure est-il?*
Do you speak English?	*parlez-vous anglais?*
money	*argent*
cheap	*bon marché*
expensive	*cher*
with	*avec*
very	*très*
thing	*chose*
United States	*États-Unis*

Chris from Chicago (USA) speaks just enough French to travel comfortably across France, but she has found that the one phrase that carries her everywhere effectively is *c'est bon* (that's good).

Numbers: Knowing French numbers helps you track how much you are spending, but raising the correct number of fingers helps equally well for indicating quantity. Americans should remember that Europeans often count one to five starting with their thumb and not their index finger.

zero	*zéro*
one	*un/une*
two	*deux*
three	*trois*
four	*quatre*
five	*cinq*

Signs: Knowing the days of the week and the other terms below will help when it comes to reading signs and flyers.

Monday	*lundi*
Tuesday	*mardi*

Wednesday	*mercredi*
Thursday	*jeudi*
Friday	*vendredi*
Saturday	*samedi*
Sunday	*dimanche*
March	*mars*
April	*avril*
May	*mai*
June	*juin*
July	*juillet*
August	*août*
September	*septembre*
open	*ouvert*
closed	*fermé*
English	*anglais*

Asking questions:

what?	*quoi?*
when?	*quand?*
where?	*où?*
which?	*quel?*
how?	*comment?*
who?	*qui?*

Food: Most menus are in French and English (often German and Spanish too) and posted in front of the restaurant.

I'm hungry	*j'ai faim*
I'm thirsty	*j'ai soif*
eat (verb)	*manger*
to drink (verb)	*boire*
drink (noun)	*boisson*
breakfast	*petit déjeuner*
lunch	*déjeuner*
dinner	*dîner*
bread	*pain*
water	*eau*
wine	*vin*
good	*bon*

bad	*mal*
hot	*chaud*
cold	*froid*

(When you see a 'c' on a faucet, that means it's hot, not cold, as in English.)

Times of the day:

morning	*matin*
afternoon	*après-midi*
evening	*soir*
day	*jour*
today	*aujourd'hui*
tomorrow	*demain*
early	*tôt*
late	*tard*

People:

man	*homme*
woman	*femme*
married	*mariée*
couple	*couple*
single	*célibataire*
undress	*deshabiller*
naked	*nue*

Places to go:

beach	*plage*
bed	*lit*
town	*ville*
post office	*bureau de poste*
campsite	*camping*
room	*chambre*
street	*rue*

Sexy French phrasebook

The type of French you are likely to hear on the swingers beach, in the bars and clubs, and at private gatherings may contain vocabulary and hidden meanings that you did not learn at school. Being able to understand what is being said to you (or asked of you) is important so you can say 'oui' or 'non' with a certain amount of conviction. For this reason, unlike the schoolboy phrasebook above, the French version of the following basic words and phrases is given before its English translation, with the suggested subtext in parenthesis.

J'ai ma règle.

I have my period. (No, I don't want to have sex with you.)

Je vous presente ma femme/mon marie/mon ami(e).

Meet my wife/husband/friend. (Check out my wife/husband/friend.)

Veuillez-vous boire l'apero avec nous ce soir?

Do you want to have a pre-dinner drink with us this evening? (If all goes well, we might be up for dinner and sex.)

Veuillez-vous coucher avec moi ce soir?

Do you want to sleep with me this evening? (I speak French as badly as you do, and this phrase is the only one I know to show that I find you attractive.)

Veuillez-vous jouer avec nous?

Do you want to play with us? (If they aren't holding their pétanque balls, assume they want to have sex.)

Vous êtes seul?

(to a man) Are you alone? (Normally means: 'Get lost!')

Vous êtes seule?

(to a woman) Are you alone? (Come to mama, baby!)

Other words you might hear:

Baiser	fuck (can also mean 'a kiss')
Bien membré	well-endowed
Bite/queue	dick
Boite échangiste	swingers club
Bouger	verb meaning 'to move'; used to describe much sexual activity at clubs and private parties
Branler	jerk off

Chatte/minou	pussy
Echangisme	swinging
Faire l'amour	make love
Fellation	blow job (also called a *pipe*—pronounced 'peep')
Femme fontaine	woman who ejaculates abundantly
Jouir	cum (verb)
Lécher	lick (verb)
Libertin(e)	libertine (people who are open-minded about and enjoy sex in all its various forms)
Mélangisme	seems to have two meanings: a) the practice of having sex next to other couples without actually swapping partners and b) swapping partners and having sex in a different room to the other couple (the strict English translation of *mélangisme* is 'mixing')
Non, merci	No, thank you (never means anything other than 'no, thank you', and should be respected at all times)
Partouze	orgy
Plus si affinités	possibility of going further if everyone gets along
Préliminaires	foreplay
Salope	slut
Sexe	male or female genitalia
Sodomie	anal sex
Soirée privée	private party
Sucer	suck
Trio or *triolisme*	threesome

About the Author

When Ross Velton (rvelton@yahoo.com) first pulled off his shorts and bared all on the beach in Cap d'Agde, all he was worried about was getting through his first day as a naturist. If you had told him then that one day he would write a book about the place, he would have sniggered. 'I'm just curious,' he would

have said. 'Once I've tried it, that's it, I won't be back.'

Tried what, exactly? The nudist beach? Well, yes, in the beginning. Then Ross, like thousands before him, discovered that the Cap was more than just a nudist beach.

His curiosity brought him back to the resort many times; and the memorable experiences he had satisfying this curiosity many times more.

This book is the sixth travel book that Ross has either authored or co-authored. He lives in Montreal, and when he is not gallivanting around nudist beaches in the south of France he enjoys flower arranging and singing in the church choir.

Quick Reference

Emergency numbers

Police: 17 (emergency) or 04 67 01 02 00
Municipal police: 04 67 94 62 20
Fire brigade: 18 (emergency) or 04 67 01 07 50
Ambulance (SAMU): 15

Tour operators

In North America

Castaways Travel—25701 IH-45 North, Suite 3A, Spring, TX 77380, USA; +1 281-362-8785; www.castawaystravel.com

LBT Limited—31 Cosentino Drive, Scarborough, M1P 3A3, Ontario, Canada; +1 416-298-0795 or 1-800-565-6795; www.lbt.ca

Through Our Eyes Travel—4452 Cypress Mill Road, Kissimmee, FL 34746-2760, USA; +1 407-870-0827 or +1 908-229-3953 (mobile); www.cap-d-agde.com

In Europe

AV Travel—UK; +44 (0)1305 767777; www.avtravel.co.uk

NatuTravel—Slenkstraat 62, 1441 MS Purmerend, The Netherlands; +31 (0)299 472174; www.NatuTravel.com

Peng Travel—86 Station Road, Gidea Park, Romford, Essex, RM2 6DB, UK; +44 (0)1708 471 832 or 0845 345 8345 (from within the U.K.); www.pengtravel.co.uk

Welcome Office at the nudist resort

Bureau d'Accueil—Quartier Naturiste, Rond-point du Bagnas, 34300 Cap d'Agde; 04 67 26 00 26

French Naturist Federation

Fédération Française de Naturisme—65 Rue de Toqueville, 75017 Paris; 01 47 64 32 82; www.ffn-naturisme.com

Apartment rental agencies

Aktys—Rond-point du Bagnas, 34300 Cap d'Agde; 04 67 26 10 68; www.aktys.com

Ann and David James (British couple who organise accommodation in Cap d'Agde)—04 67 26 03 41 (France) or 1-877-414-4038 (USA); www.capdagde.co.uk (Sometimes they rent for less than seven days)

Club Helios Husumer—Str 95, 33729 Bielefeld, Germany; +49 (0)521 76635; www.naturist.de

Geneviève—BP 883, 34307 Cap d'Agde Cedex; 04 67 26 12 62; www.genevievenaturisme.com

Peng France—BP 846, 34307 Cap d'Agde Cedex; 04 67 26 31 77; www.pengtravel.co.uk

René Oltra—BP 864, 34308 Cap d'Agde Cedex; 04 67 26 33 78; http://agenceoltra.ifrance.com

Résid'—BP 855, 34307 Cap d'Agde Cedex; 04 67 26 84 71; www.resid.com

Swingers clubs in Paris

Chez Sorlut—93 Rue des Martyrs; 75018 Paris; 01 46 06 87 02

Chris et Manu—5 Rue Saint Bon, 75004 Paris; 01 42 72 52 18; www.chris-manu.com

Deux Plus Deux—*9 Boulevard Edgar Quinet, 75014 Paris; 01 43 35 14 00; www.2plus2.net*

L'Overside —92 Rue du Cherche Midi, Galerie Le Sevrien 75006 Paris; 01 42 84 10 20; www.overside.fr

La Cheminée—11 Rue des Fossés-St-Marcel, 75005 Paris; 01 47 07 66 66

Le Bar-Bar—9 Rue Crussol, 75011 Paris; 01 48 05 76 77; www.bar-bar.com

Le Cléopâtre—19 Avenue d'Italie, 75013 Paris; 01 42 16 85 69; www.cleopatre.com

Les Chandelles—1 Rue Thérèse, 75001 Paris; 01 42 60 43 31; www.les-chandelles.com

Index

Your friends need this book

But don't share your copy—no one has ever returned it.

Your friends will be amazed about the high jinks
that go on in Cap d'Agde. Why not order a copy as a gift?
The holiday season is less than 12 months away.

Order by phone: Call toll-free 888-883-9040 (24 hrs; USA or
Canada) Visa and MasterCard accepted.

Order securely online at: www.wordcrafting.com

Order via the mail: Please make your check or money order in
U.S. dollars payable to Scarlett, Oh! Publishing.
Send name, address, payment, and quantity desired to:
Scarlett, Oh! Publishing
P.O. Box 6584
Villa Park IL 60181-6584 USA

Pricing: $22.95 U.S. each book + s/h below

USA: Shipping & handling is $5.05. Shipping each additional
book to the same USA address is $3. *Illinois residents*, please add
$1.55 per book (for 6.75% sales tax).

Canadian orders: Shipping & handling is $10.

Europe, Japan, Australia, and New Zealand: Shipping &
handling is $15.

Outside USA is $5 for each additional book to the same address.

(Shipping/handling pricing effective through March 31, 2004.)

Enjoy another book from Scarlett, Oh! Publishing:

***The Naked Truth About Hedonism II** (by Chris Santilli)*

*A Totally Unauthorized Naughty but Nice
Guide to Jamaica's Very Adult Resort*

(384 pages—32 pages in color; $22.95; ISBN: 0-9662683-3-4;
shipping & handling same as above)

For more information, write the above address or e-mail
Books@wordcrafting.com.

Thanks for your interest!

Scarlett, Oh!
PUBLISHING